# HOW TO CATCH—AND KEEP—A MAN

## (How to Love an American Man)

### By

### Donald Petty

*To Bonny*
*Donald Petty*

© 2001, 2003 by Donald Petty. All rights reserved.

No part of this book may be reproduced, stored in a retrieval system, or transmitted by any means, electronic, mechanical, photocopying, recording, or otherwise, without written permission from the author.

ISBN: 1-4107-9163-7 (e-book)
ISBN: 1-4107-9164-5 (Paperback)

This book is printed on acid free paper.

1stBooks - rev. 08/18/03

# TABLE OF CONTENTS

Dedication ................................................................................. v
Personal Note of Admonition ............................................ vii
Preface ..................................................................................... ix
    1.     How to Love a Man ................................................. 1
    2.     Seven Ways to Meet a Man .................................... 7
    3.     Nine Ways to Get a Man's Interest ...................... 15
    4.     Eight Things to Talk About ................................... 23
    5.     Twelve Things Not to Say ..................................... 33
    6.     Eleven Gifts to Give ............................................... 43
    7.     Eight Ways to Dress .............................................. 51
    8.     Eleven Things to Order at a Restaurant ............. 59
    9.     Seven Ways to Say "Goodnight" ......................... 67
    10.    Fourteen Questions to Ask ................................... 73
    11.    Eight Conversation "Sparklers" for Communicating ........................................................ 83
    12.    Nine Subjects of Interest ....................................... 89
    13.    Eight Ways to Get Asked Out .............................. 97
    14.    Twelve Kinds of Men to Avoid .......................... 103
    15.    Ten Kinds of Men to Date ................................... 113
    16.    Twenty-three Things a Man Likes ..................... 121
    17.    Thirteen Things Men Do Not Like .................... 133
    18.    Twenty-four Things a Man Likes in a Woman ................................................................... 143
    19.    Six Things a Man Does Not Like in a Woman ................................................................... 155
    20.    Nine moods of a Man .......................................... 163
    21.    Five Things To Say about Football .................... 173
    22.    Eleven Things Not to Say about Football ......... 181
    23.    Eight Things to Say about Baseball ................... 193
    24.    Six Things Not To Say about Baseball .............. 201

| | | |
|---|---|---|
| 25. | Six Things To Say about Basketball | 207 |
| 26. | Six Things Not to Say about Basketball | 213 |
| 27. | Nine Things to Say about Golf | 219 |
| 28. | Five Things Not to Say about Golf | 225 |
| 29. | Eight Things to Say about Other Females | 229 |
| 30. | Ten Things Not to Say about Other Females | 235 |
| 31. | Five Things to Say about Other Males | 243 |
| 32. | Fifteen Things Not to Say about Other Men | 249 |
| 33. | Twenty-seven Four-Word Phrases to Avoid | 259 |
| 34. | Seven Principles for Making Love | 269 |
| 35. | Ten Questions about Finances | 277 |
| 36. | Four Views on Love Held by Most Men | 289 |

# DEDICATION

This book is dedicated to the woman who will know how to make application of all the things listed in these pages. She is independent, fulfilled, busy, and only as submissive as a woman of her day is wont to be. To this day she knows "How to Love a Man." Because of my wife since 1956, I am; so to that woman who does not now agree with all that is written herein, I dedicate this book. It is to Sylvia.

## PERSONAL NOTE OF ADMONITION

The harmony brought about by the way a woman relates to a man is a result of her understanding the man, addressing his needs, selfishness, "immaturity" (childishness), and egotism in such a way that he in turn sees the beauty and value of responding to her needs and femininity.

If the two can recognize and accept the differences, strengths, and vulnerability of the other, these tips herein will endear a woman to a man for life. The surest way for this to happen is for the woman to let her head rule over her heart, as the man does, for a long while before committing to marriage (or even a one-on-one relationship).

—Don Petty

## PREFACE

Having been asked the question, "Don Petty, tell me how to love an American man," by a young woman in Honduras, I thought that to be a very intriguing question. Setting about to answer it, I tried to think what I really liked about women (and there is a lot, starting with my wife's firm independence and confident will power).

My question to myself became, "What do they say and do, and how do they look and dress, that really makes me feel good about them or close to them? My conclusions are contained in "How to Catch—and Keep—a Man."

One might do well to consider that it is written by a somewhat egotistical man who over compensates, probably to cover some lack of confidence; but that same man (with all his flaws and indiscretions) has been married since 1956 to the same tough, enthusiastic woman.

Remember, also, that the 50's marriages were committed to an entire life with one spouse, and that for the most part that was the way it was until the "sexual freedom" of the 60's and beyond.

The writer does totally and openly acknowledge that not all men will agree with the hundreds of tips offered in this book. Women by the hundreds may vehemently disagree, but it is possible that those same women may well disagree because of frustration in relationships because these very suggestions may not have been employed.

The book is not written as law; rather, it is written for women who may not have had successful relationships in dating or marriage and for young or inexperienced women who honestly want to have a good relationship with an American man.

The tips will bring a man into the world of the woman. As she does indeed sacrifice a lot of herself early in the acquaintance and relationship, she will see that it will pay dividends as the man becomes confident and comfortable with her "understanding" of him. He then commits to an equal, balanced, and generous relationship with her.

## CHAPTER ONE
## HOW TO LOVE A MAN

The average man is more interested in a woman who is interested in him than he is in a woman with beautiful legs.

Marlene Dietrich

Contrary to popular belief, sex is not the first thing on the mind of a man when he meets (or even sees) a woman he finds interesting. The first thing he thinks about is the right things, not appearing to be "hitting on" her, not doing or saying something dumb or offensive, how does he keep the conversation going (and interesting to her), and bottom line, how he will be able to see her again.

What he wants to see in her are the following things: appropriateness, looks, style, clothes, shoes, hairdo, makeup, conversation, laughs, coyness, coquettishness, actions, walk, table manners, amount of food, and attention to him with eyes, comments, body language, and gestures.

The things men are interested in hearing are not marriage talk, kids, a cottage and white picket fence, problems, bills the woman has to pay, past spouse's negatives, "macho" talk, anything about the ERA or women's rights (although he may agree with equal rights, equal pay, equal treatment), a "poor-little-me" attitude, male bashing, false praise, shallow ideas, or fantasies of life.

He would be much more interested in questions you may ask about him! Now, you've got his ear. It does not matter what at this point. It can be anything about his accomplishments or powers, hobbies, vacation, dreams, goals, his past flames, his ideas on any subject, what he likes about life, what he wants in a woman, what sports teams he likes and why, what position he played or plays on any team, his highest bowling score, his lowest golf score, when he first started dating; him, him, him.

Yes, he will be interested in any of your questions about sex and love making, romance, and dating. But he would not want a cross or demeaning attitude on sex or love.

If you show genuine passion about any topic of his interest, he will consider you nothing less than absolute greatness! If you talk about cooking, find out what he likes and let him know how well you can cook it or at any rate how much you enjoy eating it at restaurants.

Some of the type comments that build him up are such things as, "You have deep penetrating eyes. You seem to be a sensitive man. You really understand women. You know what a woman needs or wants. You seem successful without being driven by money. I bet you are a generous man with those for whom you care. You probably have a strong idea of what you want. You surely do seem to know where you are going."

Things like these get him to think and talk. You want him to talk almost as much as you do. Ask him questions, make choice comments; but be sincere with both.

You should be versatile and flexible. Plans may change without him being able to control them. He may over promise or bite off more than he can chew.

He will want to hold doors for you and walk on the street side; but he can adjust if you do not want the "southern" chivalry treatment.

He generally will not want a trash mouth woman; rather, he will want her to be above the garbage of dumbness and vulgarity and bawdiness. He wants the woman he is with to have class, so people seeing them together will consider him classy.

You may expect him to take care of you and try to anticipate your needs even before you realize you have them. If he doesn't, it's okay to tell him what you need done.

He will reciprocate your love. He will fall in love before he realizes it, but he will likely not be in love as soon as you think he is. He doesn't want "love" to get in the way of "freedom"—for him or you.

He may consider you "his girl" after one date (especially if he treats you really nice) but it's okay if you keep him posted on the progress of the relationship. If there are others you are dating or will date, it is okay for him to know that if you tell him and not let him "discover" it.

The man will like to talk and hold hands and hug and kiss. He will respect your family, but he will enjoy much more being alone with you, away from home and family.

He does not want to be rushed into commitments, nor reminded of appointments he missed. He will be there for you in your need, and he will want you to be there for him when he has a need.

Your experience in learning to love a man will be fun and challenging as well as rewarding, and should lead to marriage, home, and family.

## CHAPTER TWO
## SEVEN WAYS TO MEET A MAN

The basic discovery about any people is the discovery of the relationship between men and women.

Pearl S. Buck

Men are easy to meet; but there are certain rules to use and ways to go about it. Generally, subtlety is more effective than a direct approach.

Women are naturally blessed with a gift for being subtle and indirect. The secret is not to tip the hand and give in to the temptation to act overtly, when covertness is the path to success.

Hence, the seven best ways for an interested woman to meet a man are headlined by the most important first.

1. KEEP YOUR EYES UP. It is not impressive to the man for a woman to look down, whether it be submission, shyness, respect, fear, anxiety, or whatever. It is important to "look" so you can see him and he can see you looking at him.

Consider these advantages when you look at him. First, you see him. Look him over, watch his movements, look into what he's doing, how he walks and speaks, so you can learn about him.

Secondly, he sees your interest, and he is flattered and complimented; and your disarming him and neutralization of him has begun.

When you show an admiring interest, his desire will rise to meet you. At any point, never drop your eyes. Look equally at him, without staring; just look with interest.

He'll see your eyes up, and he'll think "she's in my world, not in a world of her own." Further, he'll feel you are ready for him to speak. Your eyes on him are already saying, "Speak to me."

If your eyes are down, they are saying, "Don't bother me." Keep 'em up.

2.  KEEP YOUR EYES OPEN. That is more figurative than literal. Paying attention lets him know you want to hear what he says, answer any question, respond to him.

He will see you as a person who is alert and with it and a current-day woman—confident and prepared. You are there! You're not away—at home or shopping or on vacation; rather, you are in the room with him, alive and in body.

His respect, even before he speaks, has already been established. He knows you are a live, warm, real body and not a wilting flower. You are at the interface and have successfully placed the ball squarely in his court.

You are established. You ARE! You really exist and stand toe to toe with him. You have not shrunk, retreated, or gone submissive. You are in the world, an equal human.

Now is no time to give away what you deserve and have just earned. Continue to keep your eyes open, not looking away, but standing in equality.

3. KEEP YOUR EYES WARM. Your eyes smile as surely as your lips. Let them loose. Let their radiance overflow into his eyes. Warm him with your warmth. Capture him with your soft, pleasant, alive eyes.

Imagine you have just received a warm fur coat, a diamond necklace, and a $50,000 bonus for excelling in your work. Now, look at him with eyes aglow. "Let him match that," you think as you warm his personality with your enthusiastic, communicating soft, and happy eyes.

Never allow the eyes to go cold or harden or narrow or waiver or weaken. They are the most important initial way to communicate. When you are ready, make the next move.

4. LOOK FOR A MESSAGE IN HIS EYES. See what he is thinking. What do your eyes say? Are his eyes warm and honest, confident and dependable?

When your eyes meet his eyes, do yours move forward? (They must not retreat.) See if his come on to see yours. Are his eyes saying something to you? Are they probing? Are they alive? Are they ready to move to the next level?

Stand your ground. Let his eyes explore and inquire without your blinking or turning or losing contact. Stay locked onto his eyes while your lips break into a gentle smile.

If this guy doesn't speak now, all bets are off. He's departed this life or he's too burdened or simple for you. Turn him loose; waste no further time.

But, since he probably speaks at this point (whatever in the world he might blurt out), be patient and controlled as you answer calmly and in total control.

5. AVOID HAVING ANY MEETING IN ANY PLACE YOU DO NOT WANT TO BE. Understand that if you meet someone in a place that is where they chose to be, it is a place they "hang out." If it is a place you do not want to be, do not be there. Get out. Whoever you may meet here hangs out at places you do not want to be. He, therefore, is not likely your type. Avoid him and his place. It's not the right place for you to be looking or expecting a meeting.

6. LOOK IN PLACES YOU WANT TO BE. If you are in a place that you are comfortable being in, you will see a man that is comfortable there, also. If you both enjoy "hanging out" there, you already have something in common.

If you meet him at church, it is a good sign you will be religiously compatible. That would be a great foundation to have to build a relationship that should grow into love.

Perhaps you are both at a concert and have an opportunity to meet. From there, you discuss the music—who you like, who you've seen. Build a platform on which you both stand and see things alike. Trade numbers and get in touch later to share some more music.

Be where you like to be and look for a man being there where he likes to be. Then when you come back there together, it will be mutually enjoyable.

7. LEARN THE ART OF LIGHT FLIRTING. This is a skill many women know from childhood; it comes naturally to them. Others do not know how to light flirt. It is well worth the time to read a book or take an adult education course.

The time invested in the course can give you two or three tips that will turn your life around. You should learn things like making eye contact, when to touch a man in conversation, how to touch him, some "little flirty" things to say, a flirty dress to wear, and probably dozens of other time-proven "tricks" to use to capture some of the time of a man you may "target."

Light flirting involves "incidental" things you might do when relating to a man. It is not to be mixed up with "heavy" flirting, which is quite different, more intense. It will be discussed later on.

## CHAPTER THREE

## NINE WAYS TO GET A MAN'S INTEREST

A woman may develop wrinkles and cellulite, lose her waistline, her bustline, her ability to bear a child, even her sense of humor, but none of that implies a loss of her sexuality, her femininity...

Barbara Gordon

Many men are interested in almost anything a woman is interested in. He shows that interest genuinely or, even if he has only a light or a passing interest, he will attempt to become interested. He will do this, first, so as not to offend you, and second, because he believes your relationship will move along better if he gets interested in your interest. In that way, you both benefit.

Men are very adaptable and resourceful, having the ability to comment on and ask questions about nearly any subject you may raise. Because of that, you can reach common ground fairly easily.

The following nine ways to get his interest should benefit you as you work to get into his thinking and become a part of his thoughts.

1. LEARN THE ART OF LIGHT FLIRTING. Once a woman touches the arm of a man while she talks to him, he will quickly give her his undivided attention. He won't really know what it means, but his interest is up, and he wants to learn why she touched his arm.

There are many little subtle things a woman can do when she employs "light" flirting, such as asking his opinion about her fragrance, her blouse, her scarf, or hair. She can look him in the eye and smile while coyly dropping her head a bit, or she can even wink when he or she says a little flirtatious word.

2. LEARN THE ART OF "HEAVY" FLIRTING. This is entirely different than "light" flirting. When she is making a strong, direct move, she may do "secret," more coercive things, like touching his foot (or even leg) with her toe.

She may comment on his broad shoulders or muscular arms or cute physique or manly body. She can tease him a bit about his "gorgeous" eyes. More physically, she may touch his face—mouth or nose or eyebrows or beard—and make a complimentary remark.

She may engage him in fairly direct, personal conversation about certain views he holds, as she explains her (possible "forward") point of view on the subject.

If you choose to be more direct by "heavy" flirting, you should recognize the potential downside. It may cause a man to think you are too fast too early or that you tend to be more "loose" than you should be. Balance your actions with your perception of what you think he expects. It would always seem to be appropriate for a woman to seek the honor and respect of the man.

3. APPLY BOTH ARTS APPROPRIATELY. In the two preceding sections, the arts of light and heavy flirting were shown to be effective ways to get the interest of the man. If they are not overdone, they can be very effective, but, as was noted, there are perils.

First, if the man perceives that you are too brazen, he may try to take advantage of you. Second, on the other hand, he may develop a distaste for the approach.

One way to prevent both is to be cheerful and enthusiastic during all conversation.

Avoid getting serious or "provocative" to the point of misleading the man. No teasing would be in order at this point. You are only getting his interest here; you are not going for a kill.

4. SMILE AT THE MAN. With certainty, you may expect him to smile back. He may even bump into a post or stumble over something to be sure that you see him return your smile, and it'll probably be his best, at least his natural smile, because he will be caught off guard if you smile before he does and not have a chance to frame it or pose or fake it.

The woman's smile opens mouths, doors, hearts, and conversations. Use it wisely and cautiously, but often and sincerely. Couple it with appropriate words or gestures or actions. You are not posing for a picture; you are simply warmly communicating to a man who you hope will respond with like friendliness.

5. SPEAK TO HIM. It's okay if the woman speaks first to the man. A simple "hello" is not out of place, nor is it "too forward" or a sign of a loose woman. If you speak, he will speak.

An unprovocative tone coupled with a nice smile and interesting, say-something-to-me eyes will not fail you. The modern man will speak and add a question most likely. He'll say, "Well, hello. How are you?" Then you continue speaking language; say, "Fine," and comment on what he is doing or something that would interest him. Now, I tell you, he does not turn and walk away at this point.

How about saying now, "My name is _____," and extending your hand. Lead on with, "I've seen you around; do you live close by?" or "I don't think I have seen you around; do you live close by?"

Now, you're cooking; turn up the heat.

6. ASK A SINCERE QUESTION. This is not a continuation of the conversation already started like in number 5 above; rather, this is an opener. A sincere question could be, "Can you tell me where the downtown bus stops in this area?" or "Can you tell me where a car repair garage is near here?" or "Is there a Chinese restaurant in this area?" or "Do you know how to get to the mall from here?"

You'll notice the litany of questions have a common thread; they are all asking for information. You are now a "damsel in distress." What (interesting) man will not help?  None of them.  So be sure you want the help of the one to whom you are posing the question.

7. MAKE AN INTERESTING COMMENT.  "It seems like I always just miss the bus," or "I can hardly wait for Cowboy season to begin," or "I sure have had a hard time following the _____ trial," or "The Hale-Bopp Comet was the most fascinating thing I ever saw; did you see it?" or "I'm ready to get home and get these feet in some nice warm water."

Note, if you make a leading comment, then follow with a question.  It will probably extract an answer.  Case in point is the "Hale-Bopp Comet comment/question in the above paragraph.  This shows him you are "current" and interested in "his view."

A negative comment doesn't do it.  Make the statement upbeat, optimistic, enthusiastic, or at least, neutral.  "Well, another week is done," or "I'm ready for the weekend."  Leave a place at the end of YOUR comment for HIS comment.

8. ASK ABOUT HIS WORK.  "Going home from work?"  "Is your work interesting?"  "Are you a big company employee?"  "Does your work involve traveling?"  "Do you drive to work?"  "Do you take the tollway to work?"  "Does your job involve overtime?"

As you ask questions, you learn about the man, plus he concludes that you are very interested in him—right conclusion!

The questions let you know his attitude toward work, if he is a good worker and stable, what his current position is, if he is climbing, or contemplating changing jobs. All these things are important to a good relationship. They all impact work stability, financial stability, and, thus, relationship stability. You want to know if he is a focused man, and these questions allow him (no, encourage him) to talk about his views on employment.

9. ASK HIM TO EAT WITH YOU. Consider all that will happen. First of all, you will enjoy a meal together, always a good time to talk and share. He'll see a new side of you, like a domestic side (not bad for him to see). The quality of your cooking will register on him, and he'll file it away for later. You can see how he handles himself at the table, and you can show him how well you handle yourself at a meal.

Should you decide to have him over to eat, ask him to go to a restaurant with you or meet you at one. Either way is fine. Even if he wants to pick you up, it's okay—your option. At the restaurant a lot of the same things apply—You learn about each other; interest is developed, and the bridge between the two of you is made stronger.

Eating together removes walls and barriers and causes a man to reveal some of himself as he really is, sort of "off guard," unpretentious. After the meal, if he doesn't say, "We'll have to do this again sometime," you should say it.

## CHAPTER FOUR
## EIGHT THINGS TO TALK ABOUT

I think the one lesson I have learned is that there is no substitute for paying attention.

Diane Sawyer

Most men are very concerned about image; primarily, they think, "What will a woman think about me?" He tries hard to make the right impression, but he wants that impression she gets of him to be both true and flattering. That is not always the way it is.

Generally speaking, men are a little too proud of themselves and boast at somewhat of too high a level. A woman need not feed that vanity, but the wisest women will talk in terms of his interest. This will pay dividends,

*Donald Petty*

as he begins to turn it around and sincerely ask after her concerns. Here's how she could do it.

1. TALK ABOUT HIS WORK. A hard working man (blue or white or GOLD collar, doesn't matter) will talk readily about the work he does. Especially will he talk quickly if he is pleased with his work and does a good job, or even if he thinks he does a good job, or even still he'll talk like he does a good job when he knows his work does not come up to the standard he likes or the company demands. The point is his work is very important to him, his image; and he wants his work to be something a woman will admire in him.

The woman interested in loving a man will learn about the man's work and learn how to talk with him about it. She might discuss with him what he does, how he likes it, his title, his position, his ambition, next step, tenure, easy part, hard part; how he got the job, how long he expects to be in it, is he satisfied or content with it; how he feels about his boss, peers, and subordinates; is he in the area he wants to be for a career, is his experience or education or training right for what he is doing?

*HOW TO CATCH—AND KEEP—A MAN*
*(How to Love an American Man)*

The questions about his work should not sound like an interrogation, but packed with genuine interest; in fact, the woman should indeed be heavily interested in this aspect of a man, as any future together may well rest on his vocation.

Money should not be among her questions—Interest? Yes, but not her questions. He will say or reveal his pay when he feels he can or should.

Interest in the man's work shows to him a woman's interest in him. It deserves a lot of communication, and preferably in an up-building manner.

2. TALK ABOUT HIS HOBBIES. Work indicates what a man has to do to support himself; his hobbies show what he likes to do, where he wants to spend his time. Hobbies are often more revealing than a man's work. He often puts more energy, time, effort, and money into his hobby than anything else. It is a real part of him and a reflective part of his nature and character.

As you talk with him about his hobbies, extend that to what the implications may be. If he fishes, realize he will get away on Saturdays and/or Sundays to be alone and fish. If you like to fish, will you be welcome or had he rather be alone or "with the boys"? What would any of these situations mean to you, to your relationship?

The same question should apply to golfing, skiing, or any other "away from home" hobby. It would be different if his hobby were collecting something. Then, the consideration of "expense" might impact the relationship. Things like racing cars or flying could be very expensive. What about that cost?

What if the hobby were gambling? Wow! Could you handle that? Yes, talk about his hobbies.

3. TALK ABOUT HIS INTERESTS. What a pity to begin falling in love with a man and you do not even know what he is interested in. Talk about education, religion, politics, philosophy, entertainment, art, museums, travel, hiking, entrepreneurship.

At this time, it is not a good idea to talk about children and marriage. These are kind of "scary" words for a man.

It is best in any relationship not to get into judgments and criticisms (even the constructive kind). Surely, a "holier-than-thou" attitude early in a relationship (or ever, for that matter) profits little and indeed may start the destruction of the relationship. It will surely impede progress.

A woman who is wise enough, early in a relationship, to talk in terms of the man's interest will find that he will reciprocate. He is interested in the woman or he would not be talking with her. He just can't communicate his true thoughts as well as she can; and his thinking, early on, is not as deep or as long-range as hers. He is thinking "surface stuff" and "now, at this moment."

4. TALK ABOUT HIS VIEW OF (SOME) SPORT. Find out what sports and games he is interested in and ask him what he likes (or dislikes) about it.

He may have played a sport in school. If he did, he will surely talk about it. Maybe if you asked him, he could produce some pictures of himself "in uniform" or "in action."

Several times through this book, it will be mentioned that the woman who asks a lot of questions in the interest of the man is wise. He will one day reciprocate, and then, she will give him a lot of "new fresh food for thought," things he never knew. She will have little surprises along for him as she lets him "explore" her past and inner thoughts and interests. This "variety" is vital for her to provide him as the relationship grows and she begins loving the man.

5.   TALK ABOUT HIS ACHIEVEMENTS. Recognition is an important need for nearly everyone.  If you can recognize what this man has achieved in his life, it will be insightful to you and very complimentary to him.  If he is a little quiet or modest, he may not readily tell you about his accomplishments.  Even if you ask him how he did in school, on the team, or at work.  Talk long enough about a subject to learn how well he did at it.  Eventually the modest man might say something like, "Oh yeah, I got a little trophy," while a more self-interested man is likely to say (before you even ask), "Oh, I got a trophy for high score in bowling," or "My promotion to district manager came after I sold $500,000 worth in three consecutive years.

In either instance, you can make him know of your keen interest in his successes (thus him) by sincerely complimenting him for work well done.  It is not a good idea to sound shallow or silly or naive by overdoing a compliment; rather, really examine what he has done and make your remarks fit his deeds.  Soon he'll be talking in terms of your success.

6.   TALK ABOUT HIS GOALS.  Do you want to know where he thinks he's going?  Or where he plans to go?  Okay, good.  Talk to him about it.  "If you could have

real success, what would it be?" "How do you define success?" "How would the ultimate success be measured in your field?" If you were able to define your view of success that is within your reach, how would you do it?"

"How would you plot a success plan in your field of endeavor?" You should discuss with him his view of his "chances" of success and what strong points he has to make it happen.

Emphasize the strong points you see in him that will help him succeed. At this time (that is, early in a relationship), stressing the positive is much more advantageous than even mentioning any negatives or weaknesses. Both could be true, but timing is everything in encouragement. As you strengthen and reinforce him, you will see how he sees the value of your help and reciprocates the efforts.

7. TALK ABOUT HIS WANTS. It is critical for you to know what the American man wants to determine if they are compatible with your wants.

It will become obvious that some of his wants are success, recognition, things (many of which would be to please you), respect, progress, and approval (yours!). He may not even realize that he has these wants, but you can talk about them in positive terms by saying things like, "Respect is a reasonable and attainable desire. When one sets his mind on it, he can determine ways to get it."

If you do fall in love with him, you need to know his "wants" in order to be able to help him gain them or, if your wants are different than his, so you can adjust your thinking or go seeking a partner somewhere else. His "wants" are probably not as easy for him to change as are his goals. His "wants" are closer to his true character than his goals. Learn his "wants" and you will better know him.

8. TALK ABOUT HIS NEEDS. What is it going to really take to make him a fulfilled man? Can you live with that? Are his needs centered in wealth, honor, service, charity, achievement, fame, being the best he can be, making a mark, rising to the top of his profession, competition, struggle, martyrdom, crusading, bettering mankind, pride, pleasing his family, religion, politics self, others? It is a varied and complicated spectrum.

In order for you to understand the real drives of the man, you must spend time with him in talk, activity, and observation to understand what his perceived needs are and what his real needs are. In his mind, they are one and the same, but are they really? Only at comfortable and relaxed times in easy conversation can you hope to learn this. Study him while enjoying him, learn his real needs and how strong his drive is to attain them.

## CHAPTER FIVE
## TWELVE THINGS NOT TO SAY

True strength is delicate.

Louise Nevelson

Some things are better left unsaid in your conversation with a man. Even if what you say is true, it can be a turn off or an "admission" that does not enhance your relationship. If he is offended by something you say, he begins thinking one of at least two things—retaliation or, "That's it; I'm getting out of here." It would seem evident that you want neither of these reactions.

There are a lot of things that will obviously not be wise to say, but the following thirteen are a wide sampling of the types of comments that may well set back your relationship.

1. HOW "DUMB" YOU ARE. Occasionally, you may be tempted to belittle yourself for a mistimed act or comment. There is no profit in putting yourself down.

You yourself will not feel good calling yourself dumb; and he will not like the weakness that term implies. Additionally, he does not want to feel he's out with someone dumb or someone who thinks she is dumb, or even someone who just says she's dumb.

It is a discredit to yourself and to the man you are with.

2. HOW "BROKE" YOU ARE. A man enjoys a successful woman as much as the woman enjoys a successful man. It is an indication to him of several things if you say you're broke; and all the things are bad.

First, he may see you as one incapable of earning enough; therefore, you must be "less than you should be." Second, he may imagine you as one unable to manage money. Third, he may perceive you as a "spendthrift." Fourth, he may consider you one easily taken by others. Fifth, he may think of you as having too much hard luck. Sixth, he may conclude that you want to use him for money. Seventh, he may take the comment as too brassy of you to ask him for his money. After all, he worked hard for it, as you must also do.

Thus, you can see, it is a no-win situation to say (or even imply) that you do not have money. Best, don't be broke; next, don't ever admit it or say it.

3. DO YOU LIKE KIDS? Most men like kids but some do not. In either case, when a woman asks that question, it sounds like the proverbial "noose" being slipped slowly around his neck. It sounds domestic, which is synonymous in some instances to "loss of freedom."

When a man is not ready to settle into a stable home life with one woman and the reality of the responsibility of children to raise, any hint of it may be enough to freeze a relationship or even end it permanently.

The discussion of "family" needs to come later, and women normally think of that aspect of a relationship before the man does. When the man finally realizes the possibility of marriage and family, the woman has probably been planning it for weeks!

Always better for him to bring up the subject.

4. I'M A FEMINIST. This comment will inevitably make him say (and probably do) something undeniably stupid!

First and foremost, he does not even know what it means, and he certainly does not know what you mean by that comment at this time to him. Confusion and chaos cloud his mind and shut down his capability to think.

Does it mean you are gay? Or like men and women? Or you just don't like men? Or you will actually look for a chance to hurt him (mentally or...ugh!...physically)? Can you be happy with him? Could you ever marry? Do you have a club of "sisters"? Are you a political activist? Whoa. What does he have ahold of here!?

Or...he may do something dumb in the other direction, emasculating men. "Yeah. Men have always mistreated women. Women deserve a better deal. I believe in equal pay for men and women. Women are as capable as men. Anything that he can say to agree he may say (and not mean it).

Even if he does agree with some (or all) of the feminist agenda, he'll still screw up his comments at this point.  It is better not to add a controversial "label" in the beginning stages of a relationship (maybe never).

5.  IT'S A MALE'S WORLD.  This is about as potentially explosive as Number 4 above.  If man does or does not have more advantages or privileges than woman, it is still an issue with land mines all in the path—avoid the comment.

In one respect, the man did not actually cause the situation that does exist; i.e. women feeling second class.  It did indeed begin in pre-history and carry up through the events of the old Bible times and into modern Oriental, Middle Eastern, Hispanic, and "red neck" cultures.

Even in all these places, it is now, and always was, a minority of people that really believe women are inferior.  Most men do not believe that and they try not to live as though they give the impression of belief.  They want to be fair, yet masculine.

Avoid the phrase, "It's a male's world."

6.  I'VE BEEN DISCRIMINATED AGAINST.  This is virtually the same as "feminist" or "male's world," but not entirely.  This does indeed happen to women more than to men in obvious ways.  It is, in fact, (almost) a stereotypical way of reaction in the business world.

*Donald Petty*

Although it is an unfortunate fact, most men will perceive you as a complainer or self-pitying or unable to compete on the real playing field if you say it. This is for conversations at better forums than in one-to-one relationships.

Discrimination is not solved in one-to-one discussions, and talking about it with a man will make for an uncomfortable evening. He will try to be interested and sensitive and consoling with his words; but he is unprepared to be of concrete help, and it will be uncomfortable for both of you.

7. I DON'T LIKE BILL CLINTON. This is political and not a good evening topic. If the man likes Bill Clinton, he will jump to his defense; if he does not like him, he'll join you and the conversation goes into negative mode. Neither direction is a winner for getting to love a man.

The thought of Bill Clinton's exploits generates strong emotions in men. Some admire him, some are turned off, some detest him, some are neutral—too many emotions for the conversation to be fruitful. Stay off political topics.

8. I DON'T LIKE ANY SPORT. Most men have sports teams. They arrange schedules based on when

teams play.  The moods of entire male populations are dictated by the way the team's last game went—he is blue and short tempered if they lost; but he is ready to take you to a nice restaurant for dinner if they win.

It is not necessary to be "into" sports, but it is essential that you understand enough for him to enjoy telling you about a certain pitch or catch or hit.  It is wise, also, to know when the play is stopped, because that's a good time to talk.

A bad time to talk is when a quarterback is about to pass for a winning touchdown or when a batter hits a game-winning home run.

It is easy enough to learn something about the sports he likes.  He'll teach you if you will learn. (See chapters 21 to 28.) Enjoy sports with him, and you'll have more time and more fun together for a longer time.

9.  I WANT TO BE A MOTHER.  At some point, it will become obvious that marriage, motherhood, and...father...uh...fatherhood...will be discussed, but it is better if the subject just "comes up," and that you have not brought it up.

Even if he is crazy about kids, he will not answer straight if he is just asked about them.  He'll bungle around 'til he has said some sort of nothing and that will even be "too much" said.

It will be a little while until he calls you again after the subject is mentioned. Keep the "motherhood" idea to yourself until he has asked you if you'll marry him.

10. THAT WOULDN'T HAPPEN IF I WERE A MAN. Whatever else that phrase may mean, it will sound sexist to the man and he'll fumble for words if you say it. It is like the "feminist" and "male's world" comments. Try to avoid it if possible.

11. A WOMAN COULD DO IT BETTER. Most men will see that as a threat. Whether it's true or untrue (and in some areas, surely it is true), he will cave in or attempt to disprove the statement. Either way, it's a loser for you and him, thus you!

It has been said, "Get a man if you want the job done; but get a woman if you want the job done right." How true, so often, how true. But it's better if the woman does not say it.

The hostile, combative mood is set once the sexist remarks are made. Once out of the mouth, they are ever remembered. The man still wants a female woman, not a sparring partner or competitor in philosophy. He seeks compatibility, not "combat ability."

*HOW TO CATCH—AND KEEP—A MAN*
*(How to Love an American Man)*

12. CAN YOU LOAN ME MONEY? The "generous" man will try to respond to the question if asked, but there are down sides that can be huge.

He will start avoiding you if he thinks you are devising ways to spend his money. Further, he will think you very brazen to ask him, and he'll question your skill to manage your financial affairs.

Nearly any other source for money is better than the man with whom you are trying to develop a loving relationship. He may even need a loan himself, though is spending generously for your dates.

## CHAPTER SIX
## ELEVEN GIFTS TO GIVE

> You may be disappointed if you fail, but you are doomed if you don't try.
>
> Beverly Sills

Gifts are appropriate on any occasion or on non-occasions. Small "remembrance" gifts that do not cost much are always appreciated by a man. He does not expect you to spend much on him, but he may spend a lot on your gifts. You do not have to match his gift.

He would be quite impressed, maybe even slightly embarrassed, if you bought him a "non-occasion" gift. It would mean a lot to him and would be a good thing to do on an infrequent basis.

Some of the things that you could give him that would be appropriate and meaningful would include the following.

1. A SINGLE FLOWER. A flower is generally what a man buys a woman, but in these days, it is highly acceptable for a woman to give a man a flower of any variety. A rose is good, a carnation, whatever your taste tells you.

The single flower shows that you like him and enjoy him and feel comfortable with him. It also says to him that you want to keep the relationship going, but not at a faster rate; "just keep it as it is."

2. TWO ROSES. Two full red roses is an excellent thing to send him if you are very happy with the relationship and want to kick it up a little, move it a bit faster, or raise the relationship to a little higher level.

Knowing that men have not historically been the flower recipient, you should understand that he will probably be surprised, but happily amazed, when he receives the two flowers. They represent you and him together in a maturing and sweetening relationship.

If you are not feeling the desire to "escalate" your time together or your feelings or closeness, it is not appropriate to give flowers. They (two) are not to be used as "thank you" or "appreciation for a good time" gifts, rather, they will be seen as the message to "move it up a notch."

3. A PIECE TO A COLLECTION HE MAY HAVE. Many men are collectors of one thing or another—coins, stamps, bottles, guns, cans, baseballs, cards, antiques, horses, bulls, or whatever. If he has shown you obvious pride in the collection and you have a good idea of the type of item and his cost range, a piece can be very much appreciated and accepted as a favorite.

If his collection is serious, it is wise to be sure your gift "fits into" the collection. If it is not one he would like, it can be awkward and embarrassing for both of you. A little research on your part will prevent an error and the gift should be a hit.

4. A NICE PIECE RELATED TO A HOBBY OF HIS. Any hobby a man might have will provide numerous gift opportunities. Most hobbies are enjoyed by using tools or instruments or sports paraphernalia and work with the hands; therefore, anything of quality that helps him enjoy his hobby is a fine addition.

The operative word, quality, will suggest research, as in "collections" above, for the correct kind. His memories of you through your gift will put his mind where you want it.

5. A GOOD BOOK RELATED TO HIS INTERESTS. All men like some kind of reading; thus, a good book that you are sure meets his reading interests will be very well accepted. One of your favorites may not be what he will read, and it will be "in the way" of your conversations. Know what you are buying; then, present it to him confidently.

6. A GOOD-LOOKING WATCH WITH A NAME KNOWN FOR QUALITY. If a man has the watch he likes, he likely will not want a replacement; but if you know his watch is not satisfactory, your well chosen one for him will be a real success.

It would not have to be an ostentatiously expensive one, but not a "cheapy" either. Good watches come from $100 on up, depending on your financial condition and what he normally wears. Not the least consideration is the time you have been together, how deep your relationship is, and where you want it to go.

Watches are tricky gifts, but the "right choice" makes for an extremely impressive gift.

7. A GOOD "MANLY" RING. Men are of many cuts when it comes to jewelry. Sometimes very macho men

like fine jewelry.  Most often, a masculine ring with a birth stone or diamond, whatever his birthday, will draw his praise and sincere thanks.

You will be able to determine what he likes by what he wears and how he talks about other men's jewelry, even if you have to draw it out of him.

If he has an empty right third finger, a ring should set well with him.

8.  A MASCULINE WALL PICTURE.  If you have seen the man's residence, you will be able to decide what kind of picture he likes.  If he has none on his walls, you may assume that photographs or paintings of hunting dogs, ships, strong statues, or (if you have queried him) abstracts of his bent, and modern art of his character, will be acceptable.

You may want to be thinking of a series to fit his decor if he has no wall picture or of matching, complementing, or contrasting with what he does have.

Any picture should be well-framed and ready for hanging when you give it to him.

9.  A WELL MADE JACKET.  Men wear a variety of jackets.  Different styles and colors and materials hang in their closets.  If you will try and find one he may be

missing in his wardrobe, you will likely have a hit with him, if you point out what he may wear it with.

Clothes are hard to get right the first time regarding the fit; therefore, offer to return it and get another if the size is wrong.

10. TICKETS TO THE (RIGHT) GAME. If you know the sports he likes and are sure of the particular game or games he might want to attend, you may do well getting (you and) him a couple of tickets for good seats. Good ones cost more, but it will be a better "treat" if he is seated (even) closer than he normally sits.

Certainly, the tickets have to be for a night when you know he is available. This gift is one that will be highly appropriate as a "non-occasion" gift. Just make it an extemporaneous or spontaneous thought. Men like that, too, when it's his kind of things.

They're a little complicated to research, but tickets to good games are most often big winners because he has fun and you participate in his interest—a win-win deal!

11. STRONG ANIMAL FIGURINES. Most men like figures showing strength, stealth, cunning, or speed. Bulls, horses, lions, cheetahs, eagles, and the like will give him a feeling of the trait for which the animal is known.

*HOW TO CATCH—AND KEEP—A MAN*
*(How to Love an American Man)*

Rabbits, birds, chickens, squirrels, or cute pigs will not do the job (unless he happens to be a collector of something like that).

Most men like to receive gifts even though you may find they will not be very expressive in the thanks. Just know inside they feel it and enjoy what you have done for them.

## CHAPTER SEVEN
## EIGHT WAYS TO DRESS

To be somebody, a woman does not have to be more like a man, but has to be more of a woman.

Dr. Sally E. Shaywitz

Men do not always have an eye for their own clothes; but they quickly recognize correct dress on a woman. It is more of an "impression" than it is a specific sight.

Your clothes convey positive, neutral, or negative vibes when a man sees you. He might not even know what he likes or dislikes, but he has a feeling of satisfaction or unease, and it affects his attitude toward you.

You know when you look at his expression how he feels. It may be a look of "WOW!" or "?" or "UH-OH," or he may be unmoved, bland. Your appearance (makeup, hair, jewelry) and your clothes set the tone of the evening or date or encounter.

There are these following considerations when you dress for a date:

1. APPROPRIATELY, ALWAYS APPROPRIATELY. You should select your dress for your own confidence, his approval, and impression on others. Give thought to what is the appropriate clothes for the occasion. Talk with him about where you will go and what you will do, so that the clothes you select will work.

If you are underdressed, it will be obvious (if not always to him, certainly to others), and things might be said to make you and him uncomfortable, hurt, or angry. The words may lead to an embarrassing scene of one sort or another.

Overdressing also may result in calling undue criticism and make you both uncomfortable. Either way, your thinking ahead of time about the proper clothes for the occasion will prevent the unneeded concerns.

It is okay to ask the man what you should wear if you are going to an unfamiliar place. He might not know exactly what you could wear, but perhaps as he describes the place and others' dress, you can determine the most appropriate outfit for you.

2. IN ATTIRE TO COMPLEMENT HIM. When a man asks you out, it is because he cares for you and wants your company. If you accept his invitation, it says the same thing about you, that is, that you want to be with him. Thus, you are a couple.

Because you are "together," your clothes should be a complement to his clothes. Your wear should not take away from his, nor should you allow his to take from yours. Your clothes should balance with his and form a complete picture.

A woman in jeans does not complement a man in a suit or even a sport coat and slacks. Neither should a girl wear an elegant black dress and pearls if the man wears only slacks and no tie or jeans and tee shirt.

It is normal for the woman to be better at clothes selection (although some men are quite adept at choosing proper clothes); therefore, you may want to take the initiative to "build him up" with your apparel and let him know how to reciprocate for your own respect and esteem.

3. "STRIKINGLY" FOR MAJOR DATES. All right! You are going to a function where everyone will be dressed! You've talked with the man with whom you will attend, and you know what he says will be correct to wear. You try to learn who all will be there and what it means to him.

When you learn that it is a very significant event for him and what it could mean to his career, you decide, "Now is the time to 'knock 'em dead.'" You have done your research, and you do not consult him anymore. In fact, he doesn't even see you with your outfit on until he picks you up to go.

At the door when he rings and you open it, you watch his eyes light up and his mouth fall open.

You have spent the right amount of time with your makeup and hair. Your perfume is at just the right intensity, and your clothes say to him, "I am all you need for this occasion."

Not exaggerating any attribute, you, in fact, downplay any specifics and let the overall impact settle in and capture his entire attention. Allowing him time to treat you in the royal manner for which you are attired, take your time to walk elegantly and ride comfortably to the location.

Enter with dignity and confidence, smiling "knowingly" and speaking firmly with grace and quiet demeanor. Look each individual straight in the eye as you extend your hand. Steady and slow, walk and talk; wait for them to come to you. Make that man you are accompanying burst his cummerbund with pride.

What you gain: There will be many such occasions for which he'll ask you to attend.

4. SURPRISINGLY! A cheerfully designed outfit on a happy, enthusiastic woman ready for an outing should provide a delightful surprise for any man calling on her. Never let him begin to "know" what you are going to look like when he comes by. Make him always wonder what you will be in when you appear at the door.

Enhance his smile with new vivacity every time he comes for you. He likes variety, not overdone or exaggerated, but slight, even subtle, changes. Sometimes he will not know what is different, but he'll be attracted by the variations.

He likes pretty and pleasant surprises in your appearance and attire—not bombshells, only minor bursts!

5. IN COLORS YOU LIKE. The colors you like depict your personality. When you wear your colors, you are more yourself—comfortable, open, fun, free.

Most men generally will go for any colors the woman likes if they are not extreme or clashing with something else she is wearing.

You will know the right colors for the occasion; thus, wear what you like in the area of color.

6. CONSERVATIVELY, around his family, bosses, customers. The last thing a man needs is for his companion to wear a dress that literally "clangs" with extremes. Pretty and quiet clothing which does not call attention nor cause irritation to a man's family, boss, or customers will help him win (or maintain) favor.

The good judgment he has in being with a woman of good judgment will add stature and credibility for him in the eyes of those present. Generally speaking, conservatism in dress is more profitable than extremism. It does not appear to be an "oversell."

7. COLORFULLY around your family. When you wear bright and colorful clothes around your family during the time a man is with you, it helps make him appear conservative. Most of the time, your family will

want your friends to be conservative as opposed to liberal or extreme.

Even after you are grown, away from home, and perhaps married, your family still feels as though conservative men are better grounded, more able to take care of you, and less likely to "roam."

On top of all this, bright colorful clothes on a woman during carefree and fun outings is usually a sign of good mental health; and that makes all of you happy—you, the man, and family.

8. DRESS ELEGANTLY on "special" occasions. If the man you are with is being honored or if you and he are attending a reception, say, honoring a friend, and you both consider it special, dress in clothes befitting the Queen's Ball.

Put everything into the quality of the dress and accessories. This is not a time to guess; rather, it is a time to be sure you are correctly attired.

Consult anyone necessary to ensure your clothes are the right ones for the occasion. It should not be left to chance. In fact, there may be only one dress that is right for you and him on this particular occasion. Be certain you are wearing it. You will know when you have

*Donald Petty*

it on. There will be only the one word to describe it. "elegance."

Dressing for a man is definitely a two-way street. When you decide you want to build up the man and in turn feel as though he is honoring you, and when you want to continually be asked out by this man, dress in a way that he is completely taken by you, your looks, your behavior, and he'll want you by his side on all occasions.

## CHAPTER EIGHT
## ELEVEN THINGS TO ORDER AT A RESTAURANT

> There have been women in the past far more daring than we would need to be now, who ventured all and gained a little, but survived after all.
>
> Germaine Greer

There is nothing quite as revealing about people as the way they eat at a restaurant. There would be a great difference in a person's eating habits at home or a fast food place and a fine restaurant (or even a good restaurant).

Your arrival at the front of the restaurant can be appropriate and elegant if you feel and exude confidence, as you allow the man to treat you like a lady. You know

## Donald Petty

you can handle yourself; allow the man to do the man things—allowing you to enter first, holding the door, gently putting his palm at the small of your back (I guess that he thinks he needs to "nudge" you inside), and saying, "Table for two please...near the window."

As you let him "seat" you, he takes on an air of accomplishment because he knows all the people saw how well he seated you. They are surely thinking, "What a cultured man."

For whatever reason, he'll want to tell you what you should have. "The poached salmon is excellent," or "You can always depend on filet mignon to be tender." At any rate, here are some ways to enhance your relationship by ordering well at any restaurant.

1. YOUR PREFERENCE OF HIS SUGGESTIONS. You know what you like to eat, but if on the early dates you try something you like best from his ideas, he will feel sure that he made your meal better. That is really what he wants, your satisfaction with the place and food he has chosen, not your praise, but your genuine pleasure.

Nearly always, he will recommend some good dishes for your consideration and you can accept or reject them; but you will enjoy a new food if you have not

*HOW TO CATCH—AND KEEP—A MAN*
*(How to Love an American Man)*

tried it before. If you have tried them and not liked them, you can always hope that at this restaurant, they'll be cooked better.

At worst, you can go ahead and eat it even if you do not like it in order not to make your companion feel unimportant. It (the evening and taste) is temporary anyway, and next time will be better.

2. A HEARTY MEAL. A man likes to see a woman enjoy eating. He thinks she looks cute, even sexy, when she eats with poise and etiquette. When she eats a hearty, nutritious, and sort of "ample" helpings, he thinks several things.

First, he believes she likes the food, thus she is happy to be there with him. Second, he interprets her good indulgence as a sign of health and vivacity. He feels she is confident with her looks and not paranoid about calories! (Besides, you can eat salads the next two days and knock off what you put on eating with him.)

3. EXCITING FOOD. He sees excitement and adventure in you if you order something that is a little (or a lot) exotic and not run-of-the-mill. Try something with a name that interests you or a dish that is pictured that looks tantalizing.

If you do not like it very much, it is still an edible food and it isn't going to hurt you...finish it. No need mentioning that you were not happy with your choice.

When you are excited and enthusiastic about your meal, it is a good upbeat impression for him.

4. NEW AND/OR DIFFERENT CUISINE. Look for something you haven't had before and perhaps something he has not eaten. Experiment and let him enjoy the new experience with you. Discuss it, what's good, what's not, what you'd change.

Compare the new dish with other ones you have enjoyed. Offer him a bite, and ask his opinion. It will be a shared experience as you determine what all is in it and how you might have added something here or there that would make it better.

5. FAVORITE DISH. Express how delicious you know something to be and order it. It will be an excellent idea to always talk upbeat about your selection and about its tastes and sensations.

It is a turnoff to speak poorly of the food or make faces of dissatisfaction. He wants to believe that you are totally content and that he has answered your every need or desire in this meal.

If you can arrange for you to have your favorite dish, he will be filled with the thought that you were fully dedicated to him for the meal. He will see your enjoyment of the food as your enjoyment of him.

6. THINGS YOU LIKE. If he is open for the evening and asks you what you'd like to eat, suggest some place you know where they serve what you like. Let him enjoy some dish that is a pleasure to you. Involve him in your tastes and the atmospheres you like. See how he likes them.

Talk with him about your times you have enjoyed the dishes and share some of your good memories surrounding the particular foods and reasons you enjoy them. Interact with him in this part of your life.

It's okay to be a little "childlike" about eating the things you ate as a child. He will be interested because it is a part of you. Get him to comment about it.

7. AN APPROPRIATE DRINK. Drunkenness is one sure way to give any man pause before he asks a woman to dinner again. The scene created when one is drunk is enough to cause most men to end a relationship.

One lady who did not drink liquor was with a man who did. A Coke seemed inappropriate; she ordered Perrier and felt quite comfortable, as did he.

*Donald Petty*

Juices, especially somewhat exotic ones, make a woman interesting and pleases the American man, not to mention they are healthy and refreshing.

8. MODERATE HELPINGS. An "overeater" is not seen by some men as a healthy or woman. They can imagine a heavy woman resulting, and most would not prefer that.

A moderately-sized dish, though it be meat, fish, chicken, vegetables, or salad, even with a light dessert in small quantity, would be viewed as a meal of a conscientious woman.

Moderation is appropriate and satisfying to most men. If she eats too little, the man might wonder if she were sickly, over-sensitive to calories, or not enjoying herself.

9. NON-EXCESSIVE AMOUNTS OF ANY DISH. Even though you select a favorite food, "seconds" would be construed as inappropriate to the man. Medium size quantities of a variety of foods would be proper.

No excess in any food or drink gives a proper indication to the man of a well balanced woman with judgment and control.

10. APPROPRIATE DISHES TO WHERE YOU ARE. Fish in a steakhouse or American food in a Chinese

restaurant would not be the best dish to order for quality or appropriateness in the eyes of most men.

If he asks you to go to a steakhouse, it is because he believes you will enjoy their steak. Should you choose fish, it will make him feel that his decision was not pleasing to you. The rest of the evening, he is feeling awkward and concentrating on trying to "make up" for his blunder.

11. SPECIALTIES OF THE HOUSE. Usually, the best prepared food of a restaurant is what they are known for—their specialty. It is normally a good choice.

The man feels good if he can order you the "specialty of the house" because he feels you are special and deserve the best.

Eating together is one of the greatest things a woman and man can do. It is time to show class and appropriate judgment. When a meal out together is a happy successful occasion, other invitations can be expected.

## CHAPTER NINE

## SEVEN WAYS TO SAY "GOODNIGHT"

"Stay" is a charming word in a friend's vocabulary.

Louisa May Alcott

Obviously, the way you say goodnight will depend on how well you feel the date went. Also, the length of time you have been in the relationship will affect you. These, however, are ways to say goodnight early in your acquaintance and "courtship."

1. OFFER YOUR HAND (SHAKE). It is never inappropriate to offer a handshake at the end of an evening where you have been pleased and things have gone well. This is especially true on a first date and other early-relationship dates. Even after several dates,

and you want to "hold" things down a little or slow the progress, you may just shake hands.

If you are into a relationship and, for the evening, things just did not feel right or progress well, or if there was a little "bump" that was unresolved and you were not totally pleased, a warm handshake will suffice.

2. OFFER YOUR HAND (FOR A KISS). If you prefer, you may extend your hand and hold it a little higher, with the back of the hand up, and an alert man will sense that a kiss on the back of the hand is right and what you want. He will kiss it in one of two ways: quickly if he is not ready to try and impress you, or warmly and slowly, if he intends to ask you out again. He perceives grace when you elegantly give him your hand to kiss.

The hand kiss is old and traditional, and can be quite romantic, exciting, and promising. With this kiss, a world of communication occurs. As always, this act must be appropriate by both involved. The action is slow.

3. EMBRACE. Even on the first date, an embrace as a "goodnight" gesture is all right. The first embrace should be slow, but short and light. Very little of your bodies should make contact on this first embrace.

This is a form of greeting and farewell the world over, and no less so with an American man. The Americans, however, read a little more into an embrace than do most peoples of the world. It is somewhat more "intimate" to the American man than other men. Early "hugs" should be short.

4. KISS ON THE CHEEK. Like the kiss on the hand, the kiss on the cheek is more of a promise than a message. It simply says, "It was a good date, and I feel good about it."

You should lean toward the man and offer him your cheek. Make clear that the kiss is for the cheek, as it is improper to have him believe you want to be kissed on the mouth, then change to the cheek.

Even if he persists to kiss you on the mouth, continue to offer only your cheek if that is your choice. A kiss on the mouth means a lot more than one on the cheek. He will prefer the mouth, and he will understand the cheek as a "slow down."

5. LIGHT KISS. After you have allowed the relationship to grow satisfactory and want it to keep moving along, offer your lips to the man for a goodnight kiss. He can wait, and you have just given him hope and a reason to call you back.

*Donald Petty*

A light kiss on the mouth is light years further along than a kiss on the cheek. The kiss is one of the most intimate acts between a man and a woman. So, be careful. Try not to get your feelings ahead of his. He may not be thinking "steady woman" when he kisses you goodnight, even when he kisses you with a long kiss that is firm or romantic.

6. FIRM KISS (CALL ME AGAIN). When you and the man have reached the level for a firm goodnight kiss, he may begin thinking there will be more physical action coming. You may not be thinking that way; thus, you will have to control the intensity of "warmth" of the emotion.

It will be wise not to let the kisses get longer, firmer, or deeper than you want. You make the decision, not him. He will warm quickly and he will repeat often. Be sure you do what you want to do. It will not likely be quite as much as he wants.

Remember, you set the pace when this is the "good night" you participate in.

7. ROMANTIC KISS (CALL ME SOON). When the woman is totally pleased with her man and the evening, she should take the initiative at the end of the date and move forward with some assertiveness to kiss the man

warmly and very romantically, not to start a fire. This aggressive kiss is to let him know that she is truly developing very strong feelings for him.

These feelings include uncommon interest, trust, comfort, security, and even the looking forward to possible love, and beyond. He must read from the kiss that there is sincere emotion involved and not just physical longing.

8. Number eight is listed here without comment because there are so many alternative ways to say goodnight. You create other appropriate behaviors and things to say. Avoid being immature at this point.

Saying goodnight is such an important part of a date. It leaves the last things on the man's mind, and he will carry away with him that night your concluding communication. Give enough thought to it to make him dwell on your message until you meet again. Enrich him with encouragement for the next step you want to take.

## CHAPTER TEN
## FOURTEEN QUESTIONS TO ASK

It had long since come to my attention that people of accomplishment rarely sat back and let things happen to them. They went out and happened to things.

Elinor Smith

It has been said that most men use only three minutes in an hour for conversation. Although they are to the point and cover a lot of territory in these short minutes, most would talk more if they were more sure of themselves. Again, most fear saying something that is wrong or sounds stupid; therefore, they just do not talk much.

You think it would be good for him and for you if he would talk more. You could learn so much more about his thinking if you could get him to open up. Although his actions speak louder than his words, and men are people of action, you both need the communication.

Here are some questions to encourage him.

1. WHAT IS YOUR FAVORITE THING TO DO? Do you see what you have done with this question? (1) You have addressed his interest. (2) You have evoked speech from him, (3) you will learn what his interest is, (4) you'll get his view of the activity, (5) you'll learn how he sees himself fitting in, and (6) you'll learn where some "common ground" is for further talk and activity. Pretty nice return for a fairly little investment, wouldn't you say?

2. WHAT IS THE MOST DANGEROUS SITUATION YOU HAVE EVER BEEN IN? Now you are calling on his imagination and giving him an opportunity to talk about courage and his appeal for your sympathy and consolation, both of which you are skilled (by nature) to offer.

You will also see what he considers dangerous and something about his activities and the way he manages them.

3. WHAT IS YOUR OWN PERSONAL SPORTS HIGHLIGHT? Now you give him bragging rights. And, although you ask him in the singular, he will likely answer in the plural. You may not really consider his answer boastful or egotistical. You may see a passion and an emotional trait come forth that you did not know he had. This just may be a button to push more than once.

Once he has told you what he did, your answer may well be, "Wow! Really?" Then, he could start off again, to repeat it or give you another one. A wise woman here will get the details of these stories and ask more.

4. WHERE WOULD YOU LIKE YOUR LIFE TO LEAD YOU? Think of the knowledge ramifications for you in this question. See what all the potential is here. You'll hear his hope and dream, his plans and desire, perhaps his steps and schedule to get there. Are the dreams and ambition realistic? Are they headed where you want to go? Can you harmonize your life with the one this American man just painted? Can you endure it,

enjoy it? Will you be a support or would you want out now?

This powerful question will provoke answers you really want to hear. Listen, and hear what the man says. You in or out?

5. WHAT IS THE HARDEST THING YOU EVER TRIED TO DO? This will teach you a lot about what his interests are, how determined he is to accomplish his goals, how he attacks difficulty, what difficulties do to him; plus he'll just talk and you'll learn about his feelings.

If he succeeded in this hard task, will he succeed again, and again. If he failed...what? Was his approach reasonable and believable? Could you have helped him? Would you have wanted to? Would you have supported him?

6. WHAT WAS YOUR MOST ROMANTIC EVENING? Wow! This one is loaded. Notice what you can learn with the answer to this question. First, you can see what he considers romantic. Whatever he thinks is his most romantic evening will give you an indication of what kind of evening you will be able to expect when he starts having feelings of "romance" toward you. Second, you can see the passion in his expression as he

*HOW TO CATCH—AND KEEP—A MAN*
*(How to Love an American Man)*

talks about this really important occasion. Third, just the sharing of the moment of significance to him is a good time for serious communication.

7. IF YOU WROTE A BOOK, WHAT WOULD IT BE ABOUT? He may have thought like so many people about writing a book about something in which he considers himself an expert. In his answer he will probably say so; then, you will know a topic of prime concern to him—a good thing for you to know. If he has not planned to write one already or has not given it a thought, you might want to allow him some time to think about it awhile. In that way, you will have an opportunity still to learn what is of primary interest in his mind.

In this question you can uncover his interest, something about his thoughtfulness and thinking patterns, and his logic. At any rate, you can enjoy a lot of talk about many of his ideas.

8. HOW DO YOU SEE YOURSELF YEARS FROM NOW? This one will be obviously packed in his eyes. He may conclude that you want to know if you are in his plans or not. He will probably include you in a significant way. It may include "still seeing each other," or in fact, it may be with you.

He may even say something about "kids." On the other hand, he may reveal a desire to be located at some other place and say he could not expect you to go with him. In any of these incidents, you gain very good insight into the relationship this man believes you have together. The question gives valuable opportunities for you to adjust your plans for the future.

9. IF YOU COULD TRAVEL ANYWHERE, WHERE WOULD YOU GO? His answers will show something about his "field of vision," how far-reaching, how widespread, how venturesome his ideas.

His answers will show something of his view of other peoples, bias or trust, fear or confidence, understanding or patronizing. It will offer the chance for you to dream a little together and share some fantasies.

On the more practical level, it will give you an understanding of how much he knows about other lands or people. All in all, his answer will give you insight about how he sees himself on the "stage of the world."

10. HOW DO YOU KNOW SO MUCH ABOUT WOMEN? This question will be seen by him as a good observation on your part, whether he considers it a compliment or flattery or just a question. He will give you some interesting "reasons."

You will hear about some of his experiences as well as some background he considers important. He will likely say some things about women that will be significant to you as you relate to him. It may cause you to want to continue the relationship or end it.

This question will allow him also to say some things he believes are "good" in a relationship and some he may consider "harmful." This will likely help you relate more easily or with more difficulty. You can then decide if there is a gap between you and him, is it narrow? Is it wide, too wide? You do want to know this as early as possible.

11. WHAT WOULD YOU CONSIDER TO BE AN IDEAL EVENING? This question does not include the phrase "with a woman" intentionally. You will want to know if he inserts the phrase himself. Certainly it is good if he does include a woman, YOU, in his ideal evening.

When he does, he will describe an evening that will likely be the outside limit of what you may ever expect. It will be the best his imagination will give him; thus, you can get a feel for the most you may expect.

If it is good in your mind and you feel it to be satisfactory, you have learned a valuable piece of information.  If it is too weak, you need to know.  If it does not include a woman at all, you may believe you will have some nights alone in this relationship.  Anyway, you can make judgments and decisions about your future with him.

12.  WHO ARE SOME OF THE MOST INTERESTING PEOPLE TO YOU?  The answer he gives you will reveal the types of people he is interested in—political, sports, celebrities, his friends, family, religion, military, workers, or whatever.  You should be able to determine if you will be compatible with his kind of thought in this regard.

Does he associate with the ones he finds interesting?  Will you be able to?  Will he want you to?  His interest in people will indicate his interests in certain aspects of life.

13.  WHAT ARE SOME OF THE MOST INTRIGUING THINGS IN LIFE?  What attracts his interest?  These things will surely be of keen interest to you.

Whatever intrigues him will almost certainly demand a lot of his time. Are they the things with which you can spend time or allow him time alone with?

You may learn that a lot of his interests are your interests.  What a great thing to know.  If you like traveling and he is intrigued by travel, you have established some terrific common ground.

14. DO YOU HAVE A "REAL, DOWN-DEEP GENUINE" PHILOSOPHY OF LIFE? Realizing that most people do not know how to answer that question thoroughly, you may have to be patient as he answers. You could even give him repeated opportunities to answer completely.

This question can extract answers that will give you long-term hope and confidence and a feeling of security. If that turns out to be the case, you can both begin working on that philosophy right away.

If his philosophy and yours are too far apart, you may be able to extract yourself from a relationship that seems to be on a shipwreck course.

As you consider these and other questions to ask a man, you will not want to be seen as an attorney questioning a witness on a stand. You will want to make the queries "flow" into the conversation smoothly and naturally.

Allow yourself to ask them only as a part of an evening together. Maybe you can stretch several questions over several dates. One evening loaded with questions can freeze up an American man, and he may feel like he is being sized up and surrounded, like prey in the eyes of a predator.

A fair policy may be to just casually drop a question among many comments of your own when things are going well and you are communicating freely and openly.

Be prepared to answer some of his questions also; because he will have some things he wonders about. If it can be a "give and take" time, both of you will gain from it.

## CHAPTER ELEVEN
## EIGHT CONVERSATION "SPARKLERS" FOR COMMUNICATING

> When I look into the future, it's so bright it burns my eyes.
>
> Oprah Winfrey

Humdrum conversations can kill an evening; too many "dead" evenings can destroy a relationship. It is wise of you to include some comments to "sparkle up" a slow-moving date. There are many things you should be able to come up with, but here are some samples that should be useful.

1. THINK OF THE MOST INTERESTING THING ABOUT BASEBALL. You have to fill in the blank, but the

completion of the comment could be something like the following:

    (a)    ...an extra-inning game.
    (b)    ...a long home run ball.
    (c)    ...an exciting play at home plate.
    (d)    ...a hitting streak.
    (e)    ...a strike out streak.
    (f)    ...a home run race.
    (g)    ...the play offs.
    (h)    ...the World Series games.
    (i)    ...game strategy.
    (j)    ...a golden glove-type fielding play.

If you choose any of these suggestions, you will want to be sure you have a good grasp of what they mean and what is currently underway as an example. Who has a hitting streak? Or who is leading the home run race?

2. HAVE A FAVORITE FOOTBALL PLAYER. Your reason for having a favorite should be real and genuine. It becomes false and paper thin if you just "pick-a-player" to like. Answer to yourself the question, "Why do I like so-and-so?" and be able to explain it to the man.

*HOW TO CATCH—AND KEEP—A MAN*
*(How to Love an American Man)*

Is the player fast, strong, intelligent, skilled, always in the "right" place, able to interview well, good looking, able to read defenses, charitable, a good family man? Learn about the players in order to have a favorite. Then talk about him, and find out how your man feels about him.

3. I LIKED THE MOVIE _____. If you know the man well enough to know what kind of movie he would enjoy hearing about, tell him about one you saw. If you do not know him well enough, tell him about some parts you liked and learn how he responds. Talk in terms of his interest until you pick up what holds his interest best; then, get on that wave length and enjoy the interaction. Expect to talk more than he does, and plan to give more elaboration than he will give.

He probably will briefly discuss a movie he has seen, or at least a part from one; but it will be a brief description and to the point. He seems to believe, as did William Shakespeare, "Brevity is the soul of wit."

4. THE PLACE I'D LIKE TO VISIT MOST IS _____. This is much like the movies, but you will speculate more and use your own imagination more explaining why you want to visit some place you may never have seen. Make your reasons good ones for wanting to see some place.

*Donald Petty*

Let him see the enthusiasm and interest you have for visiting the particular place. Determine if he knows the place and can talk about it himself. Maybe he has ideas about the same place or some similar one that he can add to the discussion.

5. THE CLOTHES I LIKE TO WEAR MOST ARE \_\_\_\_\_. Your favorite clothes may be elegant evening dresses; loose, around-the-house clothes; or beach wear. Whatever it is, tell him; then say you hope the time comes when you can wear them at some certain function with him.

Ask him how he feels about the best clothes for you to wear at places he likes to go. This helps keep his mind turned to seeking places for the two of you to go; plus you learn the kinds of places he likes to go.

6. MY FAVORITE CELEBRITY IS \_\_\_\_\_. This comment will lead to talk about a lot of characters and the performances they have done or the games they have played. You should both have a lot of stories to share on both the celebrities and their entertainment.

7. I ENJOY \_\_\_\_\_ BEST BECAUSE...! This can be any field or activity or person. You take it from here; just give some logical reasons for liking what you say you enjoy.

Seldom does the phrase "I just do" explain your likes satisfactorily. Give the guy a concrete reason he can hang on to; he does not need vague ideas. Hid mind does not work well without a clear image.

8. MY FONDEST MEMORIES ARE...! Here is an opportunity to tell him the things you are fond of. Telling him what you have good memories of in the past will let him know what you would like him to do with you in the future.

This will help him decide on places to ask you to go as well as get you to places you would enjoy. This is an excellent way to get win-win dates and a win-win relationship.

These few "sparklers" are just ideas to allow you to enjoy give-and-take communication with a man. It will certainly be more enjoyable for you if you have his honest participation in a conversation. You will get it if you talk about things he likes to talk about. It will enrich your entire interaction with him and should continue as long as you are together, even up to forty years!

# CHAPTER TWELVE
# NINE SUBJECTS OF INTEREST

Women have served all these centuries as looking glasses possessing the magic and delicious power of reflecting the figure of man at twice its natural size.

Virginia Woolf

The opposite sex is of interest to people. They were created to be so; in fact, they were designed to be interesting "for a lifetime." Thousands and thousands of couples have found interest in one mate their entire married lives—thirty, fifty, seventy years! To a man, the female gender is of utmost interest and top priority.

In this chapter, many of the interests of men are discussed. It addresses a lot of things to give you some

## Donald Petty

hot buttons of interest to almost any man. You realize the opposite sex in most cultures drives men throughout their lives. Most of their motives are impacted by the perception of the female.

The wisdom of a woman who shows total interest in the point of view of a man begins to solidify a relationship that becomes balanced, mutual, and "self-sacrificing" by both.

The wise woman continues to heed the messages and lets the interactive flow continue in a normal manner; primarily, that means speak and act and live in the interest of the man. He then begins to see the necessity of life you provide him; and he starts reciprocating your attention, interest, and love, and begins to fall headlong in love himself.

1. WOMEN. Man was made to live a productive life. It was soon evident he was incomplete and lonely and purposeless. When a woman complements him, he really gets things done and they share lives and prosperity equally. His life is lived because of her and his attention focuses solely on her. Thus from the beginning woman has been a vital part of man.

Virtually everything he does is either for her directly or indirectly. He excels because she is watching.

He gets an education to influence her and to be better able to devote his life to her security, comfort, pleasure, and success. He lives for woman.

2. GIRLS. As a youngster, he has eyes for girls. He does silly and funny things to impress "girls."

As he grows into manhood and maturity, "girls" still cause him to spend money, change plans, travel great distances, accomplish, and excel to impress them with himself.

As a middle aged man, he finds "girls" still flatter him and build him up and raise his spirits. "Girls" influence him and are of great interest to him.

As an old man, he wants to show dignity and respect and good judgment as he relates to girls. He wants to be honored and respected by girls, and he would like to counsel them.

All his life, girls are of interest and will always be a topic you can discuss with him.

3. LADIES. Most men make a distinction between "woman" and "lady." They try to see the "lady" in all women. A lady is appropriate, well-mannered, clean-mouthed, modest, quiet, and good. A woman does not necessarily have any of those traits.

A man will mix and blend with all women, but when he starts "getting serious," he will seek a "lady." When a man sizes up a female for a life-long partner and mother of his children, he longs for niceness and motherhood that will train his offspring to be good and succeed.

A "lady" is of deepest interest to an American man. She is "l'crem de l'crem"—the best of the best.

4. HIMSELF. It has been surely evident up to this point that most men are interested in, well, themselves. They are selfish and egotistical for a great part, and they really like someone to listen to their accomplishments, their danger, their courage, et. al., etc., ad infinitum.

A lot of seeds can be sown while the woman is talking to a man about himself. The questions about "him" can display her own philosophy, and she can learn what parts of his talk of himself she believes and likes or can tolerate.

She can watch for him to realize that he is talking too much about himself, acknowledge it, and turn the conversation more outward, from himself more to her interests...and he will, given enough strokes of his own.

5. SPORTS. Whether or not a man played sports (many, many did) in school, sand lot, semi-pro, or

professional, most will have interest in some sport (as well as international). Almost every man knows something about baseball, basketball, soccer, hockey, or football.

He probably knows how to play these games and a lot about his "home" (favorite) team. All you have to do is mention his team or ask him about his team. You can get him into a conversational interplay by asking which he prefers (and why)—baseball, football, or basketball.

With that inquiry, he is going off on a discourse on the merits of his favorite. Listen to him talk and learn some of his likes and dislikes, what hits some of his buttons, and all you can about his sport and his ideas about the comparisons he makes.

6. HIS WORK. Glean a lot from his talk about his work. The more he talks about his work, the more you will learn about him.

Find out if he wants to stay in his line of work or if he is not satisfied with what he does. If he is not, determine how he intends to make a change. See then if you can work with his reasoning and planned changes.

He likes to talk (good or bad) about his work. Get him to elaborate on his good things at work if he is enthusiastic about it.

7. HIS PHYSICAL PROWESS. He may like to talk about some physical feats of accomplishment. If he works out, let him tell you all about it. He'll be happy discussing it, you'll learn some things of interest, and you'll know how and what to praise about him and comments to make.

Does he work out on his own or at a gym or athletic club? Should you work out? With him? Alone? Is this common ground you can share?

Certainly, if you enjoy the interest in good health you both will more likely enjoy by working out, eating wisely, drinking a lot of water, minimizing liquor and cigarettes. All these things will lend themselves to more prowess for a longer time.

8. HIS MENTAL ACCOMPLISHMENTS. He may like to talk about problems he has solved or prevented by his quick thinking.

He may talk about his ideas, something he thought of to improve something or something he wrote.

Some high mark or good grade he received will be a nice topic of discussion. You will be well advised to learn about some of his achievements or brain skills or let him know that you appreciate a man who thinks.

9. OOPS! YOUR INTERESTS! He will not think to talk about your interests much of the time, but all that he does is directed toward addressing your interests.

He makes a big point of trying to act and talk in your terms, but he often makes blunders and oversights. But, if he knows you like something, he will bend over backwards to make it happen for you.

In fact, he probably will overdo on your behalf. Let him know you like it when he puts his attention on your interests.

## CHAPTER THIRTEEN
## EIGHT WAYS TO GET ASKED OUT

>Idealists...foolish enough to throw caution to the winds...have advanced mankind and have enriched the world.
>
>Emma Goldman

Men are often confused by women. No, that is not totally true. Communication from a woman may come in several ways; and it is certainly perceived differently by the man, depending upon whether it is positive or negative.

If a woman gives a man a negative response or reaction or answer, he may not hear it or understand it. For sure, he will usually ignore it (believing she really intends for him to ignore it). But, if the response is "yes," he immediately hears and understands. In fact, a "yes" for a pebble probably means he will take it as "yes" for a boulder! In other words, given an inch, he will try for a mile.

"Yes" is permission to escalate! He thoroughly understands "yes"; he totally misunderstands "no." Your slightest "yes" will cause him to react fairly quickly and directly. Here are some definite ways to indicate "yes" in order to have him ask you out.

1. LOOK AT HIM PLEASANTLY...A LOT! It is probable that one nice look on your part will be enough to evoke a "hello" and more. If you have given him at least three sincerely pleasant, warm and bright-eyed smiling looks, he will be thinking, "How do I keep from saying something dumb? How do I ask her out?"

You can both excite him to talk to you and calm his nerves if you look pleasant with a warm smile. It would clam him up if you shame him or tease him about the way he may approach you. Listen to his request seriously and intently and let him know his request is a good idea.

2. SMILE AT HIM REGULARLY. When he looks at you, let him see an extremely happy smile while you look at him with soft, warm eyes. Let your eyes make him know you want him to talk with you while you allow your

smile to spread shyly and a little coquettishly, not flirting; but completely sincerely.

A smile speaks stronger words than your voice. It would not be wise for the smile to appear (or become) as laughter; for that would make him start checking himself—pockets, zippers, buttons, hair, etc. He would be self-conscious. It must be a broad warm smile often to assure him you are sincerely communicating you want to move forward with him.

3. TOUCH HIS HAND AS YOU TALK. This gesture might be construed as light flirting, but it's okay, as it also conveys a degree of trust and interest on your own part. The touch of your hand on his arm will attract his complete attention.

When he looks at your warm eyes and sincere smile while you talk and touch his arm, it will be only a short time before he starts the process of asking you to eat dinner with him or see a movie or take a walk.

4. HOLD HIS ARM AS YOU TALK. This indicates that you want his undivided attention and that you are willing to offer him your complete attention. Again, as you smile and look kindly into his eyes, holding his arm, talk softly and under complete control.

Seductive comments or a sullen voice at this point would be out-of-place. Talking about any (happy) subject will be perfectly all right, but a comment about going out might not be appropriate unless your friendship has started developing. Proper timing would be the operative phrase here.

As in touching his arm, holding his arm as you talk implies your confidence with him and your trust in him. Those are good traits to hold if you are ready to be asked out.

5. TELL HIM YOU GO (SOMEWHERE, ANYWHERE)...USUALLY ALONE. You may go walking, running, shopping, swimming, surfing, skating, whatever. You may say you do these things alone, but that you would enjoy company. If he does any of those things already, you may be able to do them together and talk with each other.

At this time, you are merely "feeling him out" for his interest and to just hear his ideas about the things you do. You have given him enough at this point for him to pick up on your line of thought. Allow him some time to think about what you have said. It is not good to rush or push just here.

6. TELL HIM YOU ENJOY DINING OUT WITH A FRIEND. In the course of talking with a man, you can learn if he eats out and where, what kind of food he likes, and how often he likes to do it. After you know these things and during the conversation, you can tell him you really enjoy eating out with a friend, someone to talk with during the meal, and a companion to enjoy the evening with.

If the man is at liberty to ask you out and you have been smiling and looking at him with warm eyes, and occasionally touching his arm, this will be the opening he's been hoping for; and he'll say something like, "Well, we'll have to eat together sometime."

When he says that, you'll be prepared to say, "Soon." That may do it. He's likely to say, "How about tonight?" Be ready. If you can make it that quickly, say so. "Tonight sounds fine." If you can't go that quickly, say, "I'd like to, but can we make it some other night real soon."

7. SAY TO HIM, "IF YOU ARE AT LIBERTY...ASK ME OUT SOMETIME." This will be okay; in fact, it will be perfect. It shows you are willing, but still allows him the initiative. He will bounce around a bit, but he may ask you on the spot for a date and set a time.

*Donald Petty*

If he does not immediately do that, he'll begin thinking and planning how he will bring up the subject again soon. But, the very direct invitation for him to ask you is one of the most effective ways to date.

8. SIMPLY ASK HIM OUT. "Would you have dinner with me sometime soon?" He will say "yes" 99% of the time. He will even try to begin thinking of the day. More than that, he'll be thankful you helped him break through the "wall of fear," the fear of rejection (some say greater than the fear of death and public speaking).

This totally open and sincere way to show your genuine interest will be appreciated and very impressive to many men. This shows you like him, you enjoy his company, you have confidence, and you are strong enough to make a move. All these things he learns about you and likes.

The several thoughts on getting a man to ask you to go on a date with him basically leave him in charge, but you cause the action. This is a wise way, tested by time, for women to have what they want by giving men what they want.

## CHAPTER FOURTEEN
## TWELVE KINDS OF MEN TO AVOID

I believe that what woman resents is not so much giving herself in pieces as giving herself purposelessly.

Ann Morrow Lindbergh

A lot of the trouble women get into with men is because they pick the wrong ones. Oddly, even after they know they have picked a lemon, they stay with him. It is beyond a normal mind to understand why.

As soon as you discover you have the wrong one, "walk away." Let him know you want to go it alone and that the relationship is over.

The key is picking the right one to begin with; then, you can avoid being hurt and causing a bad scene.

Studying the man you want to interest before you let him know you want his attention.

Here are some kinds of men you will want to avoid as regards dating.

1. MARRIED ONES. There are three things that can result from you dating a married man—all bad. First, an illicit affair will cause you guilt and worry. Second, you can destroy a home and family. Third, you may win him, but what have you got? Isn't he an adulterer? Wouldn't he two-time you and leave you for someone else? His history says he could.

A romantic relationship with a married man may seem sweet in the mouth, but it is bitter in the stomach. You should never knowingly start a flame with one married, and the instant you learn he is married, end it! No explanations, no promises, no waiting—just end it! You do not want to pay the price this one extracts.

2. CRUEL MEN. Some men are cruel. This cruelty may come as a natural part of his character or it may result from training he has received. In either situation, the cruelness can, and likely will, flow over into your relationship.

Should you being together result in marriage or children, the cruelty will go on. Even if there are latent cruel thoughts in the mind of this man, they could surface at any time. Pain will result. Do not continue in a relationship with a cruel man.

3. BOASTFUL BRAGGARTS. The man that boasts is, in essence, a liar and at least a stretcher of the truth with little judgment. He is loaded with hot helium and cannot be believed nor trusted.

Let the big head practice his art somewhere else. You will enjoy better an American man with his feet on the ground, confident with reality with no "need" (perceived or otherwise) to falsely inflate himself or exaggerate his accomplishments.

If he "blows a gale," his words will always be suspect, and you'll never know if he is talking straight or imaginary. You cannot depend on him or rely on him to be there for you. Seek a better choice.

4. DESPERATE ONES. Many available men have been rejected so much that they begin feeling desperate. At that time, they start being "somebody else," trying to escape their true nature, the nature that keeps being turned away. Then they become insincere, false, and confused about who they really are.

This character, weak to begin with, becomes more disoriented and wishy washy. He will need rehabilitating and mothering and sympathy.

At best it will be a long struggle; and he will always be susceptible to someone stronger leading him away.

Your "sympathy" for such a one is not a good substitute for love. The baggage would weight you down in time. The desperate American man is one to pass on.

5. IMPATIENT ONES. The man who can potentially explode and be pushy and cause damage and get into trouble is to be avoided. Is that what you want?

It is not a given that trouble will automatically follow impatience, but lack of control can cause him to miss opportunities in his career and perhaps other situations, such as while driving or Little League. Consider the possibilities.

Even if he relates to you, it is likely you will be "too slow" or "too dull" or "too moody." Think this one through well before you're emotions get entangled.

Patient men offer some forms of security; impatient men may be reformed, but seldom do they have the patience to stick out the reforming process. His "hot head" will likely blow like a volcanic eruption, especially under stress.

6. NERVOUS MEN. The health of a nervous man is a consideration. What is causing him to be nervous—drink, smoking, diet, guilt, physical condition, stress, something upcoming?

A nervous man is likely to panic in a crisis, or abandon a post in chaos. He will be suspect on his job, and may be constantly on the move between jobs. It will be difficult for him to hold down a position. He cannot be considered trustworthy.

A nervous man may act impulsively and exhibit poor judgment. Is it worth getting into a relationship with this type?

7. CHRONICALLY OUT OF WORK ONES. There is not generally a satisfactory explanation for a man that cannot (or will not) keep a job. Without a job, a man is dependent, unable to take care of responsibilities, stripped of pride and self-reliance; and without stability. Do you want one of these?

Why would you expect to work harmoniously with a man who has no history of steady employment? If he did not take care of his single life, could he be expected to assume the burdens of coupledom? Would he carry his load (and sometimes yours in emergencies)? The answer is, not likely.

You best keep looking.

8. SECRETIVE MEN. If a man does not talk about himself and his past, he could be hiding something. The strong and silent type may be a good cliché for a Hollywood image of a leading man, but in real life you should want to hear about the past life of a man who has caught your interest.

Most men will not talk enough until you get on their subjects (women, sports, etc.), and then they will be fairly brief. But it is a big difference in normal "not talking much" and "secretive." Discern the silent gaps in the man's life and story. Get these blanks filled in before long term commitment.

9. CLINGY TYPES. Mama's boys will cling to you. They are unsure of themselves and will not be able to make decisions on their own. They will turn over the reigns of leadership to you. They will always feel second-in-line, unable to be assertive, let alone aggressive.

This lack of aggression, which is natural and innate, though requiring channeling and controlling, is a critical part of a man's character. It is important in his vocation, social life, marital life, and parentage. Be suspicious about the ability of a man who hides behind his mother's apron.

He will always want to be close to you, clinging for security, in groups and your circles. There will be a good chance for him to be jealous and hurt because of his sensitivity, even in totally innocent acts you may perform.

10. JEALOUS ONES. A jealous man will keep a microscope on you. He may even have "eyes" of others on you, and he will display a lack of trust in you. He may suspect or imagine things are happening behind his back.

This lack of trust and confidence in you may cause him such anxiety that he will do foolish things in extreme, like having you followed.

At best, he may argue with you about who you are seeing and why. Jealousy pushed to an extreme can break your spirit and your relationship. In fact, it can cause abuse and worse. Be wary of the jealous man.

11. VAIN MEN. An egotistical man is tolerable and may be considered close to normal, but a vain one exceeds the bounds of normalcy. Vanity precedes a fall. A man too tightly inflated will blow up, and all the air will go out of him. He may collapse and fall in a heap.

It is not hard to determine if a man is vain. Listen to him. Do his exploits give a true picture of him or are they exaggerated?  Do they seem impossibly super?  If they are hot air (an extreme brag), can he back them up with action or facts of truth?  Is he in a fantastic world believing in his own powers to the extent that he has lost touch with his real capability.  Does he really believe he can do the unreal?

If he has an imaginary belief that he can exceed nature, then it is a wise woman who will leave him to his own imaginary existence.

12. THE INSENSITIVE KIND.  The man you should want to choose will be sensitive to your needs, feelings, emotions, wants, and welfare.  In your conversations with him, you will learn if he cares for your cares.  If he belittles the things you think are important, if he interrupts you a lot, if he does not listen to you, if he does not want to go where you go or read what you read or see what you see, he is not sensitive.

Your intimate times will be only for his pleasure and satisfaction.  His decisions will fall out to his benefit, not yours.  He will not be aware of your pain or joy.  He will not notice your tears, your new hairstyle or dress or makeup.  He will not care about your activities.  He may just earn money, even turn it over to you, but he may not be aware that you would just like for him to turn the TV down low and listen to you talk for awhile.

If you date this kind of man, be prepared for many solitary times, even with him around. Your feelings will be overlooked by this intellectual, objective man, void of feeling. If you think highly enough of yourself, you can avoid getting ensnared by one of these guys and find happiness with a winner.

## CHAPTER FIFTEEN
## TEN KINDS OF MEN TO DATE

The way I see it, if you want the rainbow, you gotta put up with the rain.

                         Dolly Parton

In the last chapter, some men from which you should keep your distance were discussed. In this chapter, the opposite will be true; these will be the ones to go after. In order to get the men about which this chapter is written, you must be appropriate and have confidence, then project that appropriateness and self-confidence to men.

Some of the men will have many of these traits and characteristics. It will depend on you and your view to "mutually" develop with the one you prefer.

Here then are some things to look for in men you should want to date.

1. THE OPPOSITE OF THE ONES NOT TO DATE. If you make the opposite list, it would be something like the following: unmarried, kind (not cruel), not boastful, not desperate, patient, calm and controlled, steady worker, open, not clingy, not jealous (but trusting), not vain, and sensitive. Sound pretty good? Read on. Some of these traits will be expanded.

2. OPEN ONES. Any man that talks truthfully and openly about himself will be more likely to be satisfying and reliable than the secretive type. If he has a true picture of his ability and talks freely about it, without contradictions, you will learn some good things about him.

You then can reciprocate in the conversations and let the relationship grow. If he is open, you may feel content to be open with him. Neither of you need be ashamed if you can share secrets and personal history. This can solidify your relationship.

This is a great opportunity for complete and deep sincerity. The openness can make the relationship work if you both like what you hear.

3. UP FRONT MEN. Any man who is upfront, non-manipulative, and non-game-playing can make you a good date, boy friend, and husband. He is easy to understand, telling it like it is. He will be complimentary if he truly likes something, and on the other hand, he may point out errors, mistakes, or some things he does not like or think appropriate.

His "up-frontness" could become offensive to a woman with thin skin. What he lacks in tact, he makes up in honesty. He seldom "beats around the bush," but most likely will come to the point.

He does not put much stock in diplomacy and will use only a few words to give you an opinion. If you find your man to be upfront, it will be a good idea to learn what he likes and stick with it. Anything creative on your part may open you up for sharp criticism.

The man can be fun if you are not easily hurt; but he can take criticism if it is not a nag.

4. THOSE WHO GIVE PHONE NUMBERS. Normally, if you find a man who will give you day and night phone numbers, he does not have a "hidden agenda." There's not a "secret" residing with him. You can ask early on for his phone numbers and call him during the times he suggests.

Generally, a man likes to do the telephoning, but it is fine to call the numbers he gives you "just to talk" if you want. In fact, he is complimented and delighted if you call him.

He will not give you a number unless it is okay to call, so use it as he asks you to use it. If you find he is subversive about the number, be wary. Find out why; be sure he is not hiding something from you (like another woman).

5. HONEST MEN. Discuss with a man his views on honesty. How does he feel about using company assets? Does he spend a full day working for a day's pay? Does he cheat on his income tax? Is being a "little dishonest" in business acceptable? How does he feel about a "little white lie"? Will he return change if he is given too much? Will he steal? Will he shoplift? Would he return money he finds if there is a number or address with it?

If you have an honest man to date, you can enjoy him and his integrity. If he is dishonest in any matter, he is dishonest in all matters. Honesty is like pregnancy—you are or you aren't. There is not much in between. Find an honest man to enjoy life with.

## HOW TO CATCH—AND KEEP—A MAN
*(How to Love an American Man)*

6. HARD WORKER. A man who routinely works hard is generally a good man. Men are capable of hard labor and long hours. Manual labor is not always a favorite with them, but they can do it when the need is there.

Often in life the reward goes to the man who sweats. You should enjoy seeing him work and sweat to complete a hot, hard task. His rest is sweet. Though his pay may be small, he will provide and his children will love him.

Even if he works in a white collar job, he should not shirk his duty or his work at hand. You should let hard work be one of the tests you watch your mate take. Then let him know how you appreciate his labor.

7. DEDICATED ONES. It is not easy to determine if a man will be dedicated to you, home, and family; but his past history and current talk will give strong indications of his ideas of dedication (which may also be termed "loyalty"). If he is not dedicated to you, there will obviously be a question of fidelity; thus, you want a good feeling about his inclination (or commitment!) toward dedication.

Learn how he feels about his company, church, family, school, country. If he openly speaks down about those institutions, it is probable that his commitment is shallow. Would he be different toward you?

This is not a question you directly ask; rather, the answer is one you must deduce from talking with him and observing his actions. It is worth some time and effort to learn about him. You can love a dedicated man, but there will be trouble ahead if he is not dedicated to you and you alone.

8. SELF-SUPPORTING. Any man who is self-supporting, self-reliant, and independent of others is his own man. He is at liberty to handle his affairs (including a wife and family) in less-than-favorable circumstances. He has learned to face and overcome hardships, solve problems, and build a life on his own; he might be termed self-made and, thus, he is stronger, tougher, than a man dependent on others for his livelihood, decisions, or philosophy.

You will do well to date a self-sufficient man, realizing that he has made some tough choices in the past and, thus, should be able to do so in the future. If you are strong enough yourself to relate to a self-supporting American man, this can be a happy, productive, and successful union.

*HOW TO CATCH—AND KEEP—A MAN*
*(How to Love an American Man)*

9. ATTENTIVE MEN. Any man can be the most attentive man in the world. He has been taught manners and courtesy since childhood. He is educated in ways to make him be attentive to needs of a woman he is with.

He can remove outside things from his mind and address you and your needs only. You will encourage his attentiveness by allowing him to open doors, hold chairs, look you in the eye, compliment your hair, and countless other little things that are a part of gentlemanly courting.

Generally, a chivalrous man will be more attentive than one in the north; but either one can be charmingly observant when you command it, by your own dress, talk, and actions.

Attentiveness is not to be confused with sensitiveness. Attentiveness is seeing and doing, sensitiveness is feeling and responding. Both in a man are good, and you should seek and expect them.

10. COURTEOUS ONES. Most men are courteous. "Please excuse me, thank you, after you, allow me," are words all of them have been taught to use properly. Virtually all of them will use them if you cause them to do so. You use them and they will.

You display an expectation of respect and they will respond accordingly. In fact, if they do not act courteous and respectful, you may assume there is something lacking, in them or in your relationship.

You deserve respect and you may use it yourself to gain it from a courteous man. Courtesy is not faked. The man shows true courtesy when the woman he is with is appropriate and quiet.

The attributes listed in these pages may all apply to one man. If so, grab that man! If your man has these traits, the foundation is set for a solid, long term relationship.

## CHAPTER SIXTEEN
## TWENTY-THREE THINGS A MAN LIKES

It's all right for a woman to be, above all, human. I am a woman first of all.

Anaïs Nin

You will discover that men like and enjoy many and various things. In general, they like a lot of variety in people, things, and activity. Even the most conservative and withdrawn man will have more than one interest.

He may like different tasks in his work and work itself may not be among his favorite things. It's not that he is lazy or slothful; it is just that he has too many things to do to spend precious hours working!

In this chapter, you will learn of twenty-four things most men like.

1. A WOMAN OF VIRTUE. Although a most men have many likes, what he ultimately desires is a good woman with true virtue. When he is ready to fall in love, he will seek the woman he believes to be good.

He may seek interesting and fun traits in a woman, but he always wants her to have characteristics complementary to him. Finally, as he gets more and more serious about his future, he will look more deeply and feel confident of her goodness, for she will train his offspring.

High on his mind for his woman will be such traits as one he can trust, who will do him good. She will be a worker and willing to rise early to care for her family. She may have a good business head or be physically healthy and able to work into the night.

She may have domestic skills—sewing and cooking. She may know how to dress in fine clothes and work clothes. She may be a woman of strength and honor and wisdom. Her children will honor her. She will be faithful.

2. ATTRACTIVE WOMEN. The word "attractive" here does not mean beauty queen; it simply means a nice

looking person who cares for her looks and the way she dresses, has a smile, and warm eyes.

If the woman is friendly and will hold a conversation that is interesting, a man will be interested in talking with her and likely go with her.

3. APPROPRIATE WOMEN. Most men will like a woman when he sees her speak or act or handle a situation appropriately.

Among the most important things a man likes is an appropriate woman. She will look, talk, act, eat, listen, walk, and behave appropriately in all situations. This woman will be guaranteed an evening out with a man, and she will have many choices of many types of men. All of them like appropriate women.

4. ADMIRING WOMEN. Every man wants to be admired. He especially likes women when they admire him and when they make appropriate remarks of admiration.

The woman may be obvious in her admiration merely by the way she looks, and that is certainly impressive to the man; but he is blown away by her making complimentary comments about him. He likes the praise.

5. INTERESTED WOMEN. If a man is busy at work or play or planning or grooming or worshiping, and a woman is interested in what he is doing, he will find a lot of time for her and will explain in detail (as long as she wants) how, what, why, when, and where he does what he does. He likes women who are interested in him and will talk wisely and sincerely about his activity.

6. SHORT WOMEN. Tall men like short women (if); medium tall men like short women (if); and short men like women who are short (if). The "if" is assuming they are interested in him and proper with him.

Short women are never a turnoff to a man. The height would not ever cause a man to dislike a woman. In fact, short women are often extremely attractive to men.

7. TALL WOMEN. A tall woman who handles herself well and holds herself in correct posture, head high and no slumping, will be well liked.

In truth, if a man is tall himself, a tall woman will be a great pleasure for him to talk with, walk with, and go out with.

8. THIN WOMEN. Men enjoy thin women for a variety of reasons, not the least of which is when they show concern for their looks and health.

A thin woman may turn the eyes of other people—men and women; and that is always a compliment to her as well as to the man she is with. He likes thin women with good personalities.

9. FULL-FIGURED WOMEN. If full-figured women have good personalities and exude confidence in themselves and appropriate interest in a man, there will be no question—he will ask her out.

Men like full-figured women who know how to dress correctly and apply makeup modestly. If they are beautiful or not, a man will enjoy being with a full-figured woman who converses well and enjoys him.

10. DATING. One thing liked tremendously by some men is dating. Someone can come up with all kinds of fun, exciting, interesting, and pleasant things to do on a date. If a woman understands that a man considers dating one of his priorities and makes herself presentable and "dateable," she can be taken out quite readily and often.

Talk with him about dating. Learn what he likes to do and see, where he enjoys going, how he goes about it, and if he would be interesting to you. If he would, apply what you have learned and use your natural talents, and he'll ask you out.

11.  GREAT TASTING FOOD.  It has long been said, "The way to a man's heart is through his stomach." The man's heart may well be reached with great tasting food.  Most often, the taste of the food is what impresses him.  He's not very interested in food that is only nutritious and not good tasting, and he may like good size helpings and sturdy food that is protein-rich (meat, fish, chicken).

You will be well rewarded to learn how to prepare some of his favorite dishes the way he likes them, or you may serve him some of your dishes and learn if he really likes them.  At least, learn to enjoy food he likes and let him know eating with him is a pleasure.

12.  IMPRESSIVE VEHICLES.  Whether a man owns one, or sees other owners' impressive cars, he may like vehicles that are considered classics or ones with special features (style, power, value).  If you happen to be an owner of one of these, you may have an immediate bridge to the man's interest.

You may have an interest in classics yourself or you may learn some interesting things about some of them and discuss them with him with a store of knowledge.  You will likely find these things fun to talk about.

13. EXCELLENT ATHLETES. Most men have some knowledge of and respect for many sports, and they can recognize good athletes. They may know when a great play is made or a special athlete performs.

If so, you will be well advised to learn from him things about sports and sports people that he likes. You might enjoy talking with him about these things.

14. SPONTANEITY. Most men do not like surprises, but they do have fun with spontaneity. The man you are out with may decide late into a date to do something or another that neither you nor he thought would have been in the plan.

"Would you like to drive to Houston Saturday?" "How would you like to drive to Mexico with me this weekend?" "Would you like to fly to New York with me next week?" "Would you go to the basketball game with me tonight?" All of those things may be sprung on you from the mind of a man. How would you handle it?

15. SHOWING OFF SKILLS. Most men like to show off their work, handicrafts, pictures, collection, painting, curve ball, poem, novel, new cabinet he made, or anything else he made or does. They like for a woman to see some talent they may possess.

If he sings or plays an instrument, he will want you to hear him, and he will expect some positive comment. He really will like you to spend time seeing him do what he does well.

16. TOUGH GUYS. Although he may not be "tough" or ruthless or even truly athletic, he may like strong work, sports, boxing, sailing, or simple displays of power.

Energy and force and powerful action impress some men, whether by man or machine or animal or natural event. You will enjoy learning about his views on toughness and tough guys.

17. TRIPS TOGETHER. Men like to see new places, especially with an appropriate woman. The adventure of doing new things and seeing new territory with a good female companion is one activity that makes the blood run fast for the man.

The experience of travel allows time for a lot of conversation and activity together. This provides you a great learning opportunity. You will enjoy the play and see the man at play and in a guiding and leadership role.

18. PAY DAYS. Many men know a good deal about the value of money, although they may not be good

financial managers. They look forward to pay day that gives them power to buy things for a woman.

The impression he can make with his pay check is important to him; therefore, he likes pay day and experiences a little latitude of spending on that day.

19. HIS OWN ACCOMPLISHMENTS. The only thing a man might like better than his own accomplishments is sharing those accomplishments with a woman with whom he enjoys himself. He will show you his accomplishments, and he will talk openly about them. If you can enjoy hearing about them and sharing his enthusiasm about them with him, you will truly have a great time watching his boyish glee, yet serious explanations.

Talk with him and let him unload all that he has achieved; then, you can make remarks to show your happiness at his success. The bond of emotion could well grow here depending upon how well you communicate with him and how desirous you are of participating in his accomplishments.

20. SUCCESS. Most men expect success, exult in it, and are sorely dismayed when they fail. They like success far above only participating. Success has no

second place in their minds; it is only success when it is number one, first.

Most men reach for position number one, and they may not be fulfilled with anything less. A woman will gain much favor by helping her man be successful in his chosen endeavor.

21. HIS OWN IDEAS. While the education systems of the world teach students a lot of facts to remember, many men have been educated to think and create and explore and come up with new ideas. They may take delight in new imaginative thoughts, and he talks about them. They may like for people to discuss these ideas.

He is asked all his life, "What do you think about...?" Thus, he has ideas as a part of his process of existing. He, of course, believes his ideas are good and he likes them. Idea discussions and ideation (brainstorming) are good and fun and productive to his way of thinking. You will enjoy discussing the ideas he comes up with in a productive and constructive way.

22. PEOPLE WHO LISTEN. He likes good listeners who punctuate his remarks and "sparkle" him on, building onto his words. Even if you do not agree with what he says, he appreciates your listening.

If you agree, add on to his words; but if you disagree, you may choose to ask, "Have you considered this option?" or "Some might say...such and such. What do you think about it?" Then hear his comments. Listen, listen, listen, and hear. He will say things he really wants you to know.

23. PEOPLE WHO TALK ABOUT INTERESTING IDEAS. Most men tend to like people who have ideas. One time, there was a newspaper column that quoted someone as saying, "Below average people talk about people, average people talk about things, and above average people talk about ideas." Whether that is ever true or not is hard to say, but one thing is certain; most men will respond to interesting ideas.

These twenty-three things men like are good samplings of the variety of fields of interest he holds. There are many more you can discover as you begin gaining his interest, as your relationship grows.

One key operative word in the overall and general spectrum of what a man likes is variety." This does not mean surprises. Rather, it means new things revealed to him spontaneously or with build-up and preparation.

*Donald Petty*

You may enjoy a man's likes as well as he does once he let you know what they are. It should be fun for you as you learn what these things may be.

## CHAPTER SEVENTEEN
## THIRTEEN THINGS MEN DO NOT LIKE

One can never consent to creep when one feels an impulse to soar.

Helen Keller

While men enjoy life and like many things, there are things each one does not like. In this chapter, some of the key ones will be discussed. He does not express his opinion about his dislikes very much, preferring rather to just leave them alone; therefore, you will find it necessary to observe and learn by watching him what his dislikes are. He will quickly and enthusiastically tell you about his likes, but his dislikes are harder to discover.

Well, two qualified parts of that could be his work and a certain sport, but things regarding women in general or you specifically, he will not quickly, easily, or (maybe) ever divulge. He has learned to control his negative opinions about things, and he knows how to cope with those feelings. They will not likely interfere with your relationship.

Nonetheless, following are a few potential things any man may not like.

1. Pushy women. He may not say it and he may cover up his feelings about her, but inside he does not like a woman who pushes aggressively. He will not dislike her being assertive, that is, taking her share; but if she is pushing into his (or another) part, he will be nonplussed by that.

Our past thousands of years of human culture is difficult to overcome; therefore, the man (and woman) have to be aware that the fine lines between acceptability and unacceptability for both are unclear and are still being defined. Over-aggressive women can expect a typical man to not respond favorably to her pushiness.

This may be threatening to him or considered competing with him, and a woman may choose to go that route; but the suggestion here is that she tone down the pushy behavior to more of a blending tact. He will be less defensive, and the relationship will be enhanced.

2. MOUSY WOMEN.  Many men do not like for women to cower before them or show intimidation.  They like women with backbone who will stick to their guns and stand up to them (or anyone else).  A mousey (meek and servile) woman makes a man very self-conscious and awkward.  He needs for the woman to stand tall beside him, as this shows both of them to be strong and self-assured.  This makes the relationship appear strong.

This appearance will come from a mutual and sincerely respectful couple.  If both the woman and the man have pure and total respect for each other, many other characteristics will be there for them.  As time goes on, the solidity of the relationship matures and grows increasingly strong.

Keep in mind that my definition of "mousey" does not mean emotional and sensitive.  Certainly, the woman should be able to feel and hurt and cry as freely as she determines as necessary.

3. THINGS THEY DO NOT UNDERSTAND (EXCEPT WOMEN).  Normally, a man will need to understand something to like it.  He likes cars he can handle, games he can play and win, jobs he can do, trips when he knows the way, questions he can answer, puzzles he can solve, and stories he can follow.

He usually will lose patience when he cannot get "hold" of something in a reasonable amount of time. The patience of some men is shorter than others. In these cases, it is important to get to the point quickly with little buildup. He likes to understand where a conversation, for instance, is going pretty quickly.

He likes what he understands, and he needs to understand a thing before he can really like it. The better he understands a woman, the more solid the relationship, but other overriding features of a relationship will cover his lack of understanding in many cases.

4. LITTLE IRRITANTS. Many men can handle big problems more easily than little irritating hindrances. Be prepared for him to be upset by such things as a long traffic signal, a minor hang nail, a waitress being slightly slow at a restaurant, a car door that doesn't close easily, and that type of thing.

Little irritants may cause him to complain and be bothered and upset. He may even take the irritation out on an innocent party by being snippy and sharp with them.

If you can move the conversation to something totally different and more pleasant, he will stop the griping and forget the inconvenience quickly.

5. TO BE TOLD WHAT TO DO. Most men do not like their agenda arranged by someone else, nor do they like being taken for granted. Especially they do not like to be told what to do in a demanding or commanding way by anyone without authority to do so.

Even when his superior gives him a directive, most prefer being involved in the decision that leads to the order. He feels as though he is looked down upon unless someone words the directive as "agreed-to" instructions. It is much easier for him to carry out a word if he is asked, "Would you mind" doing so and so, or "How about getting" this or that done. "Can you have that in by Friday?" is better, in his mind, than "Get it to me Friday."

Minor points all, but the framing of the statement is important to him. More cooperation can be expected if he is not "told what to do."

6. CRITICISM. Usually, a man does not like criticism, even if it is constructive, positive, and for his own betterment. Men are fairly sensitive to criticism and prefer learning from their mistakes.

You may get a retort like, "If you don't like the way I'm doing it, do it yourself," if you make a critical judgment about his work or play or talk or dress or, just about, anything.

Perhaps his ego or pride gets in the way, but that is the nature of the man. Delicate persuasion may be learned, and if you use it, your relationship will be smoother.

7. UNENLIGHTENED QUESTIONS. Most men enjoy answering "intelligent questions," but have little patience with a naive question or one you should know or one he has already answered. You may pick your questions well and really try to understand the subject in such a way that his answer is meaningful and productive.

If your questions are good, showing understanding and/or intelligence (in his opinion), you will endear yourself to him, and he will take a lot of time in helping you understand.

A little "research time" on your part in the area of "good questions" will pay dividends in relation-enhancement.

8. INSINCERE PEOPLE. A man can often be fooled by an insincere woman because he himself,

generally speaking, is fairly open and straightforward. When he does detect insincerity, however, he does not shake it off. He remembers it, and the woman's credibility is gone from then on.

It seems he is tricked by the woman because he is infatuated and wants to believe and trust her. When the trust is broken, he feels the betrayal and becomes somewhat angry with himself for being naive. The hurt is hard to repair, and may lead to a (permanent) rupture in the relationship. Always, at best, he will be wary and perhaps overly cautious for all the future.

He wants to trust and he puts his trust in you, and once he is burned he may never again honor you with his complete trust.

9. WORKING WITHOUT COMPENSATION. When a man works and fulfills his agreement, he is very disturbed if his compensation is not what was agreed to. He does not easily accept underpayment for his time worked.

He may be generous during the agreement, but he is not very tolerant when one shorts him or backs out. Most consider his word as his bond, and totally expect that to be so with others.

If this is the case, he will consider your word your bond, and his agreement with you (appointment, date, or whatever) will be a non-breakable promise.

10. KIDS CRYING THROUGH THE NIGHT. Most men want something done for kids crying in the night. If they are sick, they need care, and he will help arrange the care. If they are crying because they are spoiled, he will want to stop the spoiling.

This type of irritating thing may cause him to leave and stay away. If they are his children, he usually will assume his responsibility unless you take it from him.

11. PIERCING PERSONAL QUESTIONS. A man's personal life is not always open for discussion. He may use judgments he does not care to discuss. It is a wise woman that does not push interest over into nagging.

He is private and basically silent on personal thoughts, ideas, and activities. If that privacy is invaded, he clams up and does not talk. If too often his private "space" is trespassed, he begins to stay away.

Allow him the respect of privacy. Likewise, you may expect him to give you your privacy.

12. RULE FOR THE "AVERAGE." Most rules are made by average people for average people. While all of them are obeyable, they may not be logical to all men.

## HOW TO CATCH—AND KEEP—A MAN
### (How to Love an American Man)

When they cannot see the logic, they will tend to bend, break, or go around the rule.

It will be the same in a relationship. If he cannot find the reason for something said or done or expected or demanded, he may not stick to the (your) rules.

Here is a case where agreements may be reached before taking him for granted. He may not be bound by a rule that you may live by. You may be wise not to prejudge his non-compliance. Try and understand his view and his reasoning.

13. HINDRANCES. It is difficult for some men to accept delays placed upon him. When it is time to go, he wants to go! Usually he feels the time to go is logical and easily understood. He cannot understand why you are not ready at that time. Whatever hinders you should simply be overcome or removed.

He begins to pace and make irritating remarks as time goes past the schedule. He may even be sarcastic or blow his stack. It is possible he will cancel an event or go alone if the hindrance continues.

This chapter has been designed to show some sample dislikes of men. If you can try to understand the general types of things men do not like, you will be able

*Donald Petty*

to predict and identify other things. In that way, you may avoid them and keep him in working through them.

## CHAPTER EIGHTEEN
## TWENTY-FOUR THINGS A MAN LIKES IN A WOMAN

>She must not swing her arms as though they were dangling ropes; she must not switch herself this way and that; she must not shout; and she must not, while wearing her bridal veil, smoke a cigarette.
>
> Emily Post

A man enjoys the company of a woman whether she is his wife, a sweetheart, friend, or just a companion or coworker. He likes to converse and bounce ideas off women to get their reaction. It rounds out an evening to be able to communicate with women. It is just a fuller time, a balance, for the day if a man and a woman can exchange thoughts and points of view.

One of the things a man likes best is an interesting, admiring, virtuous woman. Among the many things he likes about her are the following twenty-four traits.

1. VIRTUE. There is strong appeal in a man for a woman with high standards. Immediate respect is felt for her, and his own level of conduct is raised. The evening is pure and pleasant with no regretful aftereffects. The experiences of varieties of things follow when virtue flows between the two personalities.

The possibility of a long term relationship reveals itself in a high moral couple. Although there are other things a man likes in a woman, goodness, just pure goodness, ranks among the first.

2. ATTENTION TO HIM. Certainly, any male wants the attention of a woman. He more or less lives for that attention. She may just look at him and smile, or answer questions, or breathe praise at his wit or accomplishment. But if he has her attention, he will have a good evening.

3. LOYALTY TO HIM. A man wants his woman to be loyal and faithful to him, for the night and when they

are apart. She may verbally commit her loyalty to him or she may just show it, but in all cases he likes it when she lives it.

This makes him feel loyal to her, and he assumes himself to be a one-woman man when he knows (or is convinced) that she is faithful to him. But...the woman should expect him to say, "She is the only one," or she should not assume it to be true.

4. HAPPY COUNTENANCE. A man likes a happy face, and he will do things to cheery up her face. He will, however, do these things for only awhile. If she continues to be pouty or moody or despondent after he has made a sincere effort to brighten up her face, he will begin staying away from her unhappy countenance.

5. RECEPTIVITY TO HIS IDEAS. If a man suggests things to do and places to see, he likes it when the woman responds positively. He likes for her to like his ideas. It is much better when she responds with exuberance or enthusiasm. It is a strong put down to him if she says "no" or is reluctant. This is a little tough for the woman for awhile, because she does not want to do just what he likes, but soon he'll get her opinions and be just as excited about doing things she likes and seeing

things she suggests. (Sometimes opera and musical plays are a bit hard for him to enjoy.)

6. ACCEPTANCE OF HIM AND ALL HIS FLAWS. A man is a complete person, i.e. he has good and bad traits. With the right woman by his side, his good far outweighs his bad. He accepts his own negatives, and he likes for the woman to accept them.

It is unfortunate that a woman may set out in the beginning of a relationship to reform a man. It is usually a frustrating experience for them both. He does not like to constantly feel the pressure to correct a fault. Soon he tires of what he considers "nagging" and stays away.

7. LOOKING AS GOOD AS SHE'S CAPABLE. A man likes it when a woman makes an effort (short term and long term) to look as good as she is capable. He is made happy when she does her hair well, selects a great dress, wears the exact right makeup, applies the perfect perfume, has her nails done well, and puts on the correct amount of nice jewelry. He may not really take note of all those details. It's the "total package" he likes to look at, and he really enjoys seeing the care you have given to look as good as you can.

8. INTEREST IN LIFE. The man who enjoys life and living has great interest in many things, and he will

like being with a woman with a high interest in life. He will like her cheer and her zest for seeing as much as she can. He will enjoy discussing things of life and nature and experiences. The deeper her interest in the world in which she lives, the more pleasant will be the conversation.

9. ABILITY TO WORK HARD AT ANY TASK. It is normal for people to do a day's work, men and women. The drive and passion of some makes them able to work beyond a typical day. This trait in a woman is appealing to a man. He likes one who is durable and determined and able to work long hours when necessary. He sees in this (1) Good health, (2) persistence, (3) desire, (4) character, (5) strength. He usually considers all these characteristics good and likes a woman capable of hard work in a given situation.

10. BESIDE-HIM-NESS, WHATEVER! No matter what comes along, a man wants to know his woman will be there beside him for help, comfort, support, and encouragement. He is complete with a good woman at his side.

When she is more than a figure head, she is a full partner in the art of living and the task of life, and he will like her by his side in all situations.

11. READINESS TO ANSWER A CHALLENGE. A woman who rises to face whatever challenge confronts her is one the man will like and choose to accompany him to the ball or to the battle. If she shrinks away from the challenges of life (typical or tremendous), the man will steal away. He will see backbone and self-reliance in a woman who will counter-challenge.

12. RELAXED INTIMACY WHEN APPROPRIATE. A man likes a woman who is appropriately intimate. The appropriateness of intimacy will be difficult with married and single people. The circumstances will dictate. The operative words in the intimacy of the two are "appropriate" and "relaxed." He will not want tension or nervousness at intimate times. He will do his best to reassure the woman and offer her comfort, security, and relaxation.

13. HER BEING COMFORTABLE WITH HIM. Men do not want edgy, tense, uncomfortable women to be with them. He will try and make you feel at ease and not "jumpy" when you are with him. If you trust him as you should, you may feel relaxed and tranquil when he is with you. If you do not have the proper trust to feel comfortable after being with him a few times, you may want to re-decide your relationship. He may not be the

right man for you. You do not want to live in discomfort when you are with your man. Get comfortable or get away. He will like you more when you can be comfortable.

14. HER FEELING SAFE WITH HIM. He likes a woman who feels as though she can let her hair down with him and not imagine she will be hurt mentally, physically, emotionally, or socially. He wants you to be safe and know you are safe with him. He will take care of any dangers around you, and most importantly, he will cause you no harm. He likes it when you let him know you feel safe with him.

15. HER ADMIRATION OF HIS "SKILLS." Any man likes his strokes. When you sincerely praise what you have seen him do or heard him say, he likes the accolade. It may be public or private, but the most important compliments come from you.

It is the wise woman who knows when, how, and what to praise in a man that lets him know she is aware and appreciates his skills.

16. HER (SINCERE) COMPLIMENTS. Specific compliments are considered to be approval by the man, and he does continually need the approval of a woman. It cannot be empty flattery; it must indeed be praise you

really feel. Otherwise, it will begin to show through, and that "false" praise is worse for his ego than no praise at all.

When you compliment him, you reinforce his actions, and he will continue and even improve himself because of your positive reinforcement. Sincerity is key when you praise him.

17. HER INDEPENDENCE. He wants you to be independent, able to stand on your own feet, and go it alone if it is ever necessary. He does not want a woman that is so dependent upon him that she is lost when he is not around. She must be able to fend for herself. This frees him to work the hours he must or in the location required without worry for her welfare.

This is good for you also because you may feel confident with your own ability to make it on your own if it is ever needed. This must help you "self-actualize," i.e. realize your own potential.

18. A "CAN-DO" ATTITUDE. When you are positive, you can support a hard-driving man as he is pushing in his work. After a long day, he does not need pessimistic or negative input at home or on a date.

If both of you are working, neither of you need to put down the work, each other, or anything else for that matter. The attitude should be "nothing is too hard for us if we stick together and never give up." He will like that attitude.

19. SUCCESS. The successful man likes it when you succeed. He wants you to be successful at what you attempt. This would be true as a wife and mother, employee, volunteer, teacher at church, whatever! If you choose to do it, he wants you to succeed.

As much as he likes being a winner, he wants you to be a winner. He finds as much delight in his woman being good at something as he does himself. It just continues to show his good judgment in going with you.

20. SPUNKINESS. Get-up-and-go, self-starter, initiative, or spunkiness, all the same, and he respects it. He wants you to be quick to react to any situation and to react appropriately and decisively. He may not be impressed with a namby-pamby effort or pussy-footing around. He wants to see you pounce if the time to pounce presents itself. He likes for you to stand up for your beliefs with dignity.

21. FEMININITY. Boy, does a man ever like a soft, very feminine woman, especially when he knows there is a tough woman inside that feminine exterior.

The more feminine the strong woman can be, the more masculine will be the man she chooses to be beside her. The male-female balance is attained when the tough, feminine woman and the strong, sensitive man become a team, a friendship, a couple. He likes feminine women.

22. TASTE IN DRESS. Not only does a man admire the good taste of a woman selecting her own clothing, but he likes to ask her opinion about his own judgment when he buys his clothes. He appreciates her opinion of both, and he likes being asked his idea of what she selects to buy and to wear at various functions.

He likes for her to have definite likes and dislikes in clothing. He may not like for her to try and keep "in fashion" just to be in fashion. He likes for her to have her own fashion opinion, even though he may be happy for her to know what fashion circles are dictating.

23. GIVING MORE THAN IS NECESSARY. This might be termed a generous spirit or an abundant attitude; but whatever it is, a man likes for a woman to give beyond what is required.

He usually will in turn do the same with her, and he really enjoys doing it for her. It is just doubly nice when they both offer well over the need without keeping score. It's a win-win-win deal—a win for her, a win for him, and a win for them.

24. RECEIVING HIS GIFTS WITH EXPRESSIVENESS. Some men really like giving gifts and expect responses as much. He knows the giving of gifts is done with careful consideration and with a lot of thought and emotion. He wants them to be appropriate and well-received. He knows from the expression if he was successful or not—it affirms his judgment and he likes that.

Many things liked by men were pointed out in this chapter. Certainly, there are more you can imagine to do and to create yourself. He'll like a lot of things you do if you have him in mind when you do them, although he may never have heard of them before. You think of things to do that he'll like based on your knowledge of him gained by time and observation. Then do them, say them, give them! He'll show gratitude, and your relationship will grow.

## CHAPTER NINETEEN
## SIX THINGS A MAN DOES NOT LIKE IN A WOMAN

> One is not born a woman, one becomes one.
>
> Simone de Beauvoir

Sometimes a relationship that should develop just doesn't. This is often because one part of the couple or the other does not like something about the other part. This chapter is intended to point out some things that a man does not like in a woman. If you know this in advance and do not have the desire to change, that is fine. If you do want to change for the man, that is okay, too. Merely having the knowledge of a potential dislike will offer you options.

Here are six things a man does not like in a woman.

1. MASCULINE ENVY. Clearly, the man likes femininity in a woman. That is enough. He dislikes masculinity in a woman if it is self-induced. It is quite another matter if the woman has some natural male traits. The American man can often cope with that.

An example of self-induced masculinity is the woman journalist who talks like a man, often clenching her jaws and sounding as if she has a mouthful of sand. Another example might be a woman taking on a typical man's job just to prove a point. Again, it is different if she truly has a sincere passion to do the job. At any rate, the man seldom sees masculinity in a woman as something he likes. It seems to him that it is almost a confession of inferiority complex if that woman tries to be like a man, as not many men try to be like a woman.

Comfort in her own role makes him comfortable in his own role. He does not respect masculine envy by a woman. She has no reason to envy a male; she is complete in herself by being a total woman. He likes her as a woman.

2. MALE BASHING. He does not like to hear a woman bash males (generic). He may well agree with her

view of one (or even some) particular male(s); but he is highly offended if he is included in a stereotype which does not fit him.

If he is not a "good-for-nothing, two-timing male," he does not want to be grouped with them. If he has not abused a woman, he is not pleased at being categorized as "all men abuse women." If he has not been unfaithful to his wife, he does not want to be grouped with those men women say are "all unfaithful." He does not want to be classified with those men women say, "whose tongues hang out when a 20-year old, bikini-clad, bronze beauty queen prisses by." (Well, in honesty, only a blind guy would not see her, but his tongue hanging out? Don't think so.)

When a woman says, "They ought to all be hung by their toes and beaten," that is male bashing. When a women's organization or any feminist says "Men are animals and are all rapists," that is male-bashing. A man does not like for a woman to take part in that; and it is a pretty sure thing he will get away from that situation pretty soon.

3.  INCONSIDERATION. Men are believed to be more inconsiderate than women but that is not always the fact. If a man has bent over backward to make a

woman a total woman and has supplied her needs and many of her wants at some expense of work, time, or money, he really wants (deserves?) consideration.

Even if he is accused of a wrong-doing, he deserves to be heard. If he has done something wrong, his apology and/or explanation should be heard and given consideration. However, that is not always the case. An inconsiderate woman may seize an opportunity like the above to "even the score," and give him no consideration. In that case, he dislikes the act entirely, he resents what it means, and if he has tried to reconcile it without success, his feelings (love?) wanes and he will move to get out of the arrangement. Man does not like inconsideration.

4. SELF-PITY. A man has very little patience with the self-pitying woman (just as she should have none with his self-pity). At this point, she may realize males have some problems, too; although, nearly any male will admit women do have more, yes, even many more than men do. But, in neither situation, is self-pity any part of any answer. It serves no purpose, and he completely dislikes it.

Self-pity indicates to him that the woman is either (1) weak, feeling sorry for herself, or (2) trying to manipulate him by playing on his emotions. In either situation, it is certainly something he dislikes in a woman.

5. FAKINESS. A man knows women sometimes fake things, and he also confesses he doesn't always know when; but when the "fake" becomes known, it reduces credibility and trust in that area (as well as in others). Faking is dishonest; and a woman is either honest or dishonest. She (like men) either lies or she doesn't lie. Faking is lying. He does not like fakiness.

The woman will do well to try to be truthful in all relations with a man. It is better to openly discuss a problem with an intent to reach a solution rather than sweep it under the rug, pretend it is not a problem, and hope it goes away. This will be true in all aspects of a relationship.

6. HOT/COLD, ON/OFF-NESS. One characteristic of people is mood swings; yes-no pendulum; hot on an idea one day, cold the next; yes, then no; on and then off. These things are hard for a man to contend with. He doesn't know what to expect.

Although it has been laughed off as a woman's prerogative to change her mind, it is not really a laughing matter to the exasperated, confused man. He acts befuddled and dumb because he does not know what the woman wants. It is a moving target, and he is at a loss to know where to aim. Even into strong, really-long-term relationships and marriages, this changeableness continues, and the frustration continues. The man is led to spout off something dumb and hard and cruel and cutting because he just does not know which woman will show up.

It may be said that "all women are Geminis, the twins"; but in those who do not believe in astrology, this is not an acceptable conclusion. There are a lot of left brain women (i.e. objective, logical thinkers) who also have this tricky little trait of mood changing or "permission-revoking."

Like a young, talented sports team, you really never know what may happen. Or like the shape-shifters of Star Trek, the "mood-changers" appear in different forms. The man can only guess who's likely to show up.

It is easy to imagine the chaos in a man's mind as he tries to plan an evening, or a trip, or...a lifetime (?) When the mood may shift on an unannounced schedule.

A man does not like the on-again, off-again trait of a woman.

Primarily, a man would disklike a woman absent of virtue, inattentive to him, disloyal to him, unhappy appearance, unreceptive to his ideas, and so on. But the summation of both chapters, Eighteen and Nineteen, is that you learn what he likes and what he dislikes. If you can live with it, go for him. If you cannot handle it, look elsewhere.

The other option, and the one with the most challenge (and potential fun) would be to adapt your life to his, modify your lifestyle to his. Then, without your being the sculpture, allow him to very slowly adapt his to you. The fun will come in the molding of your lives to meet somewhere in between.

One wise lady (my wife) said, "You have your circle, I have mine, and we share a circle in between." The fun circle is the one in the middle.

## CHAPTER TWENTY
## NINE MOODS OF A MAN

> It's not the men in my life, it's the life in my men.
>
> Mae West

"Moodiness" is a term used to describe a typical, accepted-as-normal woman; but a moody man is thought to have an emotional problem. For straightening the records, a man is moody, too; he just doesn't reveal it as readily or in the same way. He tries to conceal it, in fact.

A man is an emotional creature. He has a share of right brain (subjective, artistic, emotional) thought. Some few have more right brain influence than left brain.

At best, whether weak influence or strong, every man has distinct moods. The nine most significant of these include:

1. DEEP THOUGHT (RAREST OF ALL). Occasionally, a man will display a pensive demeanor. He is not really daydreaming; he is more likely considering a decision (past or future). He is contemplating the perceivable ramifications. He does not have many of these period; thus, he is in unfamiliar mental territory.

Now, he may do a lot of critical thinking, but it is not the same as deep subjective thinking, where the answer is vague, not black and white. It doesn't pop out at the end of deductive reasoning.

Because he cannot "reason" it out, he wrestles with it. The thought may cause unrest, lack of sleep, somewhat erratic behaviors, and a faraway look. He is not "at himself," and he will act, be, and talk with a somewhat different attitude and personality.

There is probably not any particular thing you can do for him to get him through the thing; but knowing that it sometimes happens may help you better understand him and assist in your loving him.

2. NAIVE HAPPINESS. Often a fully grown and truly mature man may take on traits of boyhood. This is

likely to manifest itself in a flag football game, at a party, in the swimming pool, or in the car (when he feels challenged by a cool motor at a stop light).

He will revert to his adolescent mind, even in the thick of a momentous business occasion, a heavy pressure decision time, or on vacation or a weekend off. No rhyme or reason is necessary; if the mood strikes, he just goes with it.

So much the better for you if it happens to show up as a youthful amorous release of tension or pent up emotion. The best way to handle it is enjoyment, go with the flow, avoid fighting it. Get caught up in it yourself, and let other important things go. This is important, also.

If he's happy, enjoy the naivete of it. Join in with him.

3. ANGER. Even controlled men get angry. Anger is a defined mood and emotion. Explosive anger is a dangerous thing; while an anger well-channeled and in-harness may be a plus, preventing an explosion!

The downside is that anger at one thing spills over into other things. It affects the man's thinking and rational judgment, and may cause actions that will later extract guilt or repentance or regret.

If you can let him vent a bit of the anger without taking personal offense, it will be better for both of you. It will subside.

But try to make it unacceptable enough that it does not become habit-forming and happen too often. When you see the "rage" mounting and you have tried to help him vent it, but it still boils, go to the grocery store, or for a drive (or stroll), or even go to a movie, and give him time to cool off.

If dinner is delayed an hour or two while he rants or seethes, it might cause a little thought next time before he flies off the handle.

But leaving him alone on your part should not be framed as a punishment; rather, it is just something for you to conveniently do. You are not the one to confront him or settle him or straighten him out. He will have to do that. He will learn to assume the responsibility for quenching his own fire. Your responsibility is to just not add fuel to it.

4. SPONTANEOUS ADVENTURE. One mood is summed up by his saying, "I just want to go somewhere, somewhere we have not been." This is an adventurous mood and can be fun for both of you. Join him. Get

things ready; maybe even jump at the idea. You want spontaneity? Here it is. Capitalize on it.

This is a not-too-well-thought-plan he may conceive; therefore, when you can, build in some safety nets and pop off valves. Have some options and alternatives in your own mind, preferably less-expensive ones. He has probably overloaded his posterior with his mouth.

You may want to call ahead for conditions or reservations. You may even want to try to get in some maps and instructions or some sightseeing brochures.

However, if you are just driving around and he says, "Let's go to (somewhere, anywhere)," just hang on for the ride. You may wind up having to buy a new toothbrush, and you could be lucky enough to wrangle a new outfit out of it wherever you stop because he probably didn't think about needing them.

Let him have fun, help him have fun on his adventure. It would not be good to discourage this spontaneous behavior.

5. GENEROSITY. This (or these) may not be psychologically-defined moods but if he has a generous notion, enjoy, but help him not overdo it and regret it. If you do spend too much, it may not happen again. If you

control the spending and temper his mood, you may be considered wise and stable; and you will stand a good chance of it happening again.

Anytime a man's generosity is exploited, it hurts your future chances. Every time you spend less than he offers or anticipates, your future chances are enhanced. Does that not seem logical?

A generous mood indicates a generous man. Maybe you will recognize what you have and not kill the goose that lays the golden eggs. You are well advised not to manipulate this mood; rather, enjoy it as an extra benefit, not a regular stipend.

6. TOP OF THE WORLD. A man gets on a high peak quite easily. A raise or promotion will do it. A choice bit of praise at the right time from you may do it. His own success at something coupled with a Dallas Cowboy victory over Green Bay may do it. A large royalty received can do it. Whatever puts him on top of the world, the results are the same—he feels great and upbeat.

Now is a nice time to talk with him about himself and his interests and needs. He'll likely turn it around to your needs, or maybe better, the positive aspects of your relationship.

Whatever, nothing should be forced to a conclusion during this high time; but you want to couple with the exultant feeling some mention of a pending decision. Planting a few seeds during a good emotional high, and after a delicious meal, may be wise. Again, no pressing for a decision now would be in order, as it may be revoked during a downtime. But some simple talk will not hurt.

Associating what you want with his good times is a nice way to reach a win-win agreement down the road. He'll like it, and so will you.

7. DEEP BURIAL. A truly despondent mood of a man may occur as a temporary thing. This may come on at the loss of a parent, child, family member, friend, or boss, or other death. It may be at the failure of a business, loss of a job, a transfer, or a career-changing event.

All will result in the same thing, a withdrawal and a feeling of despair. An obvious change in outlook, even physical appearance may result. He is not making any mountain out of a mole hill; it is real and he is at a loss to correct it. Then, all your tact and support and encouragement skill will be needed. Do nothing to be in the way or any kind of impediment. Do everything to paint the brightest realistic picture possible.

Any scrap of positive news or opportunity might ease him over a tough bump. Even if you are feeling it, too, be optimistic and upbeat. Paint rainbows and flowers, not storm clouds and rain.

This deep burial of himself within himself will take time. Your friends could be called on to come over often or ask him over. The more worth he feels, the quicker he will tend to snap back. Make him know he is valuable.

8. FEAR. The mood of fear is real but curable with work. A man fears little, but sometimes taxes, public speaking, and death become paramount. Then fears are overcome when the event is passed, taxes are paid, speech is made, death is stayed.

When there is a tax problem, help him work through it; if it is public speaking, offer to hear a practice; if it is a fear of a death-dealing verdict or prognosis, be there when he receives it. The answer may be life instead of death. Keep him thinking that way. Fear is usually a temporary mood.

9. VICTORIOUS. A mood of victory prevails when a game is won, a week is done, a mortgage is burned, don't you see? This is a happy time, somewhat like the

"top of the world" mood; therefore, celebrate! Make plans for a victory party!

Blow it out big! If it is a time to party, make it a grand one. Invite a bunch of friends. Let him know his victorious mood has not fallen on deaf ears. If he is in a victorious mood, a time of rejoicing and celebration should be known and enjoyed by all.

Honor him at the get together, have a friend toast him; stand by him; get pictures; make it a day he'll remember. Record it on tape or photograph for posterity. Your man made a major accomplishment, and his victory face is on. Join him in the glee.

All these moods and quasi-moods go in to making up the mind of a man. These subjective feelings coupled with his logical, intellectual, objective feelings make the whole thinking man. The woman of his eye is well advised to know he has these moods and make appropriate responses for them.

## CHAPTER TWENTY-ONE
## FIVE THINGS TO SAY ABOUT FOOTBALL

A woman can do anything. She can be traditionally feminine and that's all right; she can work, she can stay at home; she can be aggressive, she can be passive; she can be anyway she wants with a man. But whenever there are the kinds of choices there are today, unless you have some solid base, life can be frightening.

          Barbara Walters

Most men like some sport or other. Of those men, the majority like football. Therefore, a woman wanting to know how to love that man should learn to love what he loves. You need to know about football.

The man will really enjoy your getting involved with him in the game, either watching at home or even going out to see a game. When you do sit with him to view a game, there will be times to talk and times no one should talk.

For example, when an explanation is being made about a penalty, i.e. when "a flag is down," that is not a good time to talk. However, when a commercial is being shown, that is a good time to talk.

The real question is "What should you say during a game?" This chapter will give five answers to that question.

1. HOW DO THEY KEEP IN MIND ALL THOSE PLAYS? He'll give you an answer, but it will be smoke, because he really doesn't know the answer to this one, but it will challenge him anyway, and he'll think of you as being a smart football watcher.

All through the game, he will be adding to his answer as ideas come to him about the plays. You just keep nodding positively and saying, "Oh," "Uh huh," "I see." This is not a good time to press. (After all, what do you care? Right?) Just accept his explanations in stride and keep on watching and bringing popcorn, tortilla

*HOW TO CATCH—AND KEEP—A MAN*
*(How to Love an American Man)*

chips, lunch snacks, and his favorite beverage to the viewing area for you and him to enjoy.

During the game, you really do not want to be caught napping or reading. This is rude and certainly very near "sports sacrilege." After all, if the networks have gone to this much trouble to bring the game to you live with sixteen camera angles and instant replay, three or four times on every play, you should surely return the favor by seeing every play, shouldn't you?

Just a little tip here, as you catch a quick glimpse of the man sort of talking to himself about all those plays, you may grin a little, but not so he sees it.

2. THINK OF HOW MANY WAYS THEY CAN SCORE. This is not really an innuendo, but you may think of it as a little private joke while he enumerates all the ways.

There's the extra point for one point, the safety for two points, the field goal for three points, and the touchdown for six points. With combinations of all these, a score of anything over one is theoretically possible for a final game score.

"One point" is not possible because the point after (or extra point) can only be made after a touchdown has been made for six points. When you see a score of, say,

Donald Petty

twenty-one to nothing, you can generally figure one team has scored three touchdowns (six points each) plus three extra points (one point each) or three times seven, twenty-one.

All this heavy arithmetic tells a lot about the game. You will amaze him if you know how to discern scores. You may even want to ask him point blank how much a safety is worth. (By the way, it is two, as is a pass or run for a score after a touchdown—seldom used, but it will grow and become a part of the strategy.)

3. I WONDER IF THERE ARE MORE RUNNING TOUCHDOWNS THAN PASSING TOUCHDOWNS. This is kind of a thought question for him. He doesn't really know, but it'll make him think.

He will respect the comment at least, and he'll think about it a lot in days to come. The best thing is that you are into his element, and he sincerely likes your being there. He'll share it all with you. In fact, you'll hear more than you ever really wanted to know, but go ahead and listen. It'll pay off.

Not only will you know more about the game, but the bonding between you two will reap its own kinds of rewards. Besides, you may learn to like the game; then, you can drop the prepared questions and become spontaneous, asking deep philosophical football questions because you truly want to know, even as one with an inquiring mind.

4. WHICH IS THE BETTER, A STRONG OFFENSIVE TEAM OR A STRONG DEFENSIVE TEAM. This one has a short answer (defensive); but he should not be let off that easy. Ask him, "Why is that so?"

Then, he will give some not-too-solid answers; but it's all right. Listen and learn. Learn about him, how he handles a question about something he knows little about, but has just heard sportscasters say for years. "Defense wins championships."

He doesn't know why, but he thinks he does, and that's good. Accept his explanation and build on it. "Which position is the most key one on defense? What are defensive 'keys'? Are there many defensive sets? How do they know which defensive play to call? Why do teams have differing defensive philosophies? Is there a favorite one? A best one?"

You can have a great time with defense. Get the questions down and let him really get into it. He'll be buzzing for weeks to his buddies about defense. He will even take on a new appreciation for defensive play.

*Donald Petty*

5. HOW DO THEY DETERMINE WHICH TEAMS ARE IN THE SAME DIVISIONS?  He generally cannot name even the teams in the Dallas Cowboy's division (and they are "America's Team"). Rarely can a man name all the teams in all the divisions, and to him, it is not important and does not matter.

The fact that you asked the question, however, changes everything! Now, it is important. "Whatever her reasons for asking that question, I want to get her the answer," he thinks.  "She really is into this!" he concludes, however erroneous or however true.  He may have to grab a paper and look at all the division teams.

He will explain that half are in the American conference and half are in the National conference.  The champs from these two conferences will play in the Super Bowl in January.  The winner then will be crowned, "World Champs."

He will then explain that his team is in the East Division of the National Conference.  And he'll gloss over a list of irrelevant ignorance by saying something like, "They determined who was to play in 1997 by the win-loss records of 1996." That is calculated to both put you in awe at his wisdom and satisfy your curiosity regarding the question.  But, your question does not have to be answered, and you already know the level of his intelligence and wisdom; thus, you're left with the result you intended—communication with him about an interest of his. Bingo. Success! You win!

This chapter gives you some football facts and insight, and ways for you to get into another of his interests. You are part of it, in partnership with your man. There are absolutely no losers here. Thus the chapter gives you important data for your mental documentation. It revealed some comments to talk about during commercials.

## CHAPTER TWENTY-TWO
## ELEVEN THINGS NOT TO SAY ABOUT FOOTBALL

I am never afraid of what I know.
Anna Sewell

While a woman may ask some very good questions or make excellent comments about football to a man, there are some definite things not to say because they will give him an impression that the question or comment was shallow or that you are spoofing (teasing) him about a game that may be dear to him.

All of the good you build up with brilliant comments can tumble down flat with one wrong comment. Observe well and long before speaking at all. Think through the words you will drop before him for his reaction.  This may provide one great education when the words you choose sink into his oval-ball-saturated mind.

Following are some things not to say.  They are representative samplings and not all encompassing.  The territory is too vast and ripe to be completely covered and harvested.

1.  WHAT IS A TOUCHDOWN?  If you ever ask this question, it is all over!  The guillotine falls.  You may as well turn in your chips, for the overly full-figured lady has sung.  This one is anathema, because this is what the game is all about—scoring a touchdown.  A touchdown is when the football is carried or passed (completed) across the opposing team's goal line, or when it is "covered" (by a body on the ground) in the opponent's "end zone."  This is, pardon the expression, the guts of the thrill, the object of the offense and the dream of the defense, this, dear lady, is the separator of the tough and the puff.  Read and re-read the touchdown definition in this paragraph.

You may ask what a safety is or a touchback, or even a first down; but never what a touchdown is!

2.  WHAT IS A P.A.T.?  This question can be answered again by just watching.  The P.A.T. (Point after touchdown) is referred to as the "extra point," "the point

after," "the point following the touchdown," "the point." All these are understood.

Always an attempt to get the extra point after a touchdown (TD) is made, most always by kicking it through the posts of the goal posts, but sometimes it is a rush for the two points after.

The running points after have just been in the game a few years. It actually is worth two points if it is made. The rule has made the strategy somewhat different when obviously you can get more points (if needed) with a little higher risk of getting none.

The P.A.T. is not a done deal after a TD; it is sometimes missed, but rarely. It is liked strongly by some "purist" fans, but a lot of viewers would like to dispense with it as it is not a "thinking" part of the game. (The kick versus the run P.A.T. adds a slightly new dimension.)

No need to ask what the P.A.T. is now.

3. WHAT DOES "OFFSIDES" MEAN? A man will explain this to you once. He will not want to tell you again, because it is simple to explain and easy to grasp; but you really do not want to "waste" his first (and only) explanation. It should not be asked.

Donald Petty

You can learn enough right here to understand thoroughly and never wonder again. Both teams have sides (or goals to defend). They are at opposite ends of the playing field (sometimes referred to as the "gridiron." Have you ever heard such a manly word?)

They always work with their backs to their goal, their "side" is always behind them. The opponent's side is always in front of them. They line up facing each other, their side behind them.

If a player crosses the imaginary "line" between opposing (300 lb.) linemen before the ball is handed (between the legs of the "center") to the key man called the "quarterback," they are said to be "offsides." The line between the big opposing linemen is termed the "scrimmage" line, and everybody has to know where it is. (What? I don't honestly know how they know where it is, they just do…They're paid to know. Trust your writer, they know!)

Thus, if any player crosses the scrimmage line from their side (behind them) into the opponent's side (before them)—from anywhere on the "gridiron," they will be called for a rule infraction. A yellow "flag" will be thrown onto the ground, and they will be assessed a penalty. The penalty will be "walked off" back toward

*HOW TO CATCH—AND KEEP—A MAN*
*(How to Love an American Man)*

their side behind them. If it is five yards, the official marks it off and "spots" the ball at what is now the new, imaginary, "scrimmage" line.

Okay, now that the "offsides" call is cleared up, read on. Do not ask what "offsides" means.

4. WHICH ONE IS THE QUARTERBACK? Taboo. Another taboo question. Quickly be sufficed, the quarterback takes the ball from between the legs of the center and throws it to somebody, hands it to somebody, gets knocked down with it, or takes off running like a scared jackrabbit. You'll know the quarterback.

The quarterback is THE MAN! He gets forty to fifty million dollar contracts. He is the field general. He (and only he) can say smart things to the papers about the owners (not the coaches, mind you), the owner or owners.

The quarterback makes the team "go." He "leads" the team. If they go to the Super Bowl, he led them. If they don't go, he failed them. He is the 370 lb. Lineman's target. He alone gets "sacked" (i.e. slammed to the ground), all others get "tackled." He is a "pinpoint passer" or he throws "lame ducks." He is on-target or off-target. He moves the team or is ineffective.

He "commands top dollar" or he is on his way out. He is always fodder for the newspaper sportswriter. He is a role model, a hero, a community treasure; or he is a goat, a disappointment, or a "bad image for our children."

He is addled "because of all those concussions." He is tough, tall enough, and strong. He can "scramble" or he is a "pocket passer." He is the focus of wrath or the hope of the team. He is the future or he represents the past.

He is a franchise player or the team's weak link. He is the central figure on the field. He is the one that is "going to Disneyland" at the end of the Super Bowl. He is on sitcoms, but can't act. He is a "smeller" of goal lines, a "sensor" of red dogs, a "reader" of blitzes, and a "glutton" for punishment.

Now, you know this super man; never ask again.

5.  THEIR PANTS ARE TOO TIGHT. First, you mustn't even notice. They are tight because it makes them run faster, and it makes it harder to hold on and tackle them. The tightness is designed in for tactical reasons, not for fashion or viewer appeal.

What this comment does is reveal a lack of understanding of the priorities of the game. The statement is not unlike what male football fans have heard said for decades by female viewers of the game. It is not unexpected, but it doesn't have to happen. It does not raise the happiness level of the man.

6. WHY DO THEY PAT EACH OTHER ON THE REAR? This is a question that is better left unasked because it is simply answered by saying, "It's a football habit of encouragement or congratulations." It is not really common in other sports. It is the "high five" of football.

It is not a sexual thing; it is the deepest way to give quick praise and confidence. "We really needed that play," or "We really need this play." That is what it means and all it means.

Where it came from apparently is not known. It goes virtually unnoticed by pattee and patter alike. It is the communication of the athlete that is noticed. The question borders on "meddling" with the "sacred cow," football. Don't ask it.

7. HE CAN'T THROW VERY WELL, CAN HE? The short answer to the question is, "Yes, but he is off today." Your man may answer in frustration, "No. They ought to set him down!"

But the real truth is that he is a professional NFL quarterback, and that fact makes him a good passer. It just may not be clicking for him for a variety of reasons. The point is that the question is not a good one because his (overall) skill is not questioned.

The question could be phrased more on this order, "Is he as good a passer as Troy Aikman?" or "Is he as good at passing as he used to be?" Those two would probably work to your advantage. But you, a rank rookie viewer, can absolutely not question the wisdom of the NFL coaches in matters like the passing skill of a quarterback. You just aren't qualified.

8. THE COACH SHOULD SIT DOWN AND BE QUIET. Well, first that will not (cannot) ever happen. Secondly, you just can't possibly have thought through what makes a coach walk and talk on the sidelines. Third, it is essential that the coach get his message to the team and officials.

What you do with that question is literally tear at the fabric of football. Coaches walk and prance and rant and, sometimes, get upset with the officiating. Occasionally a player will make a minor error and the coach will tell them about it (ever so gently, don't you see?)

The coach knows the game, his players, and what they are trained to do in all situations. His players are not doing it, and he wants them to know he has noticed it. So he tells them. In reality, he has already spoken to them as a gentleman in comforting tone, but now (due in part to crowd noise), he has to raise his voice a bit.

As he walks then, you will note, he takes on a sincere, cherubic countenance as he speaks to the heavenly beings on the gridiron. You will do well not to interfere with the divine machinery.

9. I THINK HE'S SHOWING OFF, DANCING LIKE THAT AFTER HE SCORED. The observation again is accurate, he is showing off. In reality, he is only doing what he is paid to do, i.e. running, hitting, and crossing goal lines; but he does enjoy the freedom to celebrate a victorious moment.

This is an area where the nation indulges the athlete by rejoicing with him as he creates the new victory dance. The NFL big wigs spent many man-hours years ago simply to determine if the celebrations should be allowed or not. In their collective "infallible" wisdom, they decided, "it stays!" Therefore, you cannot question it.

10. HOW MANY POINTS DO THEY GET FOR A FIELD GOAL? Three. That's the answer. Three. You need never ask again, it does not change. It is a tenet of the game, the field goal will always be in the game, and it will always be three points.

These types of questions are givens and can be determined by merely observing the game and watching the scoreboard. The basics are scoring, running the ball, passing, blocking, and tackling. No questions should come up about the basics that cannot be handled by a passing remark, such as, "His running is beautiful to watch," or "He blocked the guy right out of the play," or "his passing is right on the money." But direct questions (What does it mean to block? What is a tackle?) surely need to be avoided.

11. I DON'T THINK THOSE CHEERLEADERS ARE SO HOT. Wash your mouth out with soap. They are! Never say the cheerleaders are not hot. Most men believe the cheerleaders are vital to the game of football. Their only complaint is that they are not on screen enough.

The color added by the hundreds of cheerleaders around the NFL spice up the game a bit. Not many people cheer with them, but they add the pageantry needed at a game. They represent the colors of the team and do some worthwhile charity and publicity events on behalf of the team.

They do work hard and they do practice a lot to get the routines down, but again, you are right. They contribute nothing to the game, and in truth, they are only tiny drops in the ocean. They are kind of an entity unto themselves, but they help girls travel and have fun, and careers have even been launched by scouts seeing them perform.

They are club "good will ambassadors." Therefore, do not make derogatory comments about the cheerleaders.

This chapter has tried, in a business sort of way, to educate you further about football and to furnish you with ideas of things not to "tread on" and specifics about what not to say to the man about football.

## CHAPTER TWENTY-THREE
## EIGHT THINGS TO SAY ABOUT BASEBALL

She openeth her mouth with wisdom;
and in her tongue is the law of kindness.

*Proverbs*

Baseball is a better-known sport than football. Girls raised in the United States probably had opportunities to play ball, although chances are, it was softball and slow pitch. Still, the basic rules are similar. If, on the other hand, a girl was raised in an environment where no ball was played, the terms and rules will be virtually unknown.

The things mentioned here to say to a man will be useful to all readers as they try to learn to love a man who is a baseball fan. There were some tongue-in-cheek comments regarding football (although the suggestions were serous).  The same may well be true in this chapter on baseball.

It is possible for you to learn a bit about baseball as well as some ways to be involved with your man as he enjoys the "favorite American pastime."  You, too, will be able to enjoy the enhanced relationship.

Here, then, are eight things to say to a man about baseball.

1.  HE COVERED THAT NINETY FEET PRETTY FAST.  This would be a dazzling statement just after a batter ran past first base, whether he got there safely or was put out, if it were a close play and the runner was obviously trying very hard to "beat out" the hit.

Does that language sound foreign?  You will speak it soon if you will watch the game and learn the objects of hitting and defense.  Like football, there is offense and defense.  Offense comes when players are at bat; defense is when the players are in the field, and their pitcher is on the mound throwing the ball to the batter.

There are ninety feet between all bases.  From the home plate to first base is ninety feet, and so on around the diamond.  First to second is ninety, second to third is ninety, and third to home is ninety.  Thus, in order for a runner to score, he runs a total of 360 feet.

If he hits the ball and gets to first safely, he has hit a single; if he gets to second on his hit, it is a double; and to third, it's a triple; and to home, it is a home run or homer.

If he really runs fast from a base to a base, you can say, "He really covered that ninety feet fast."

2. HE HAS A WICKED CURVE. This is not talking about his character or the shape of his body; rather, this is a reference to the way the ball turns on the way to home plate. The word wicked means extremely good; it curves a lot. If you make the statement, "He has a wicked curve ball," it means the pitcher really can throw a good curve ball, one that makes a curve in the air on the way to home, so much of a curve that the batter may swing and miss the ball entirely.

Now, the only way you can make that statement is if you actually can tell the ball is curving when he pitches it. You will need to watch him throw awhile and catch the movement yourself. That way, you actually see it, and you will probably agree "the pitch is mean."

He will really perk up if you are able to see the curve and make that "very baseball" comment.

3. HE MUST HAVE HIT THAT THING 400 FEET. The normal home run hit is about 330-360 feet. When it

is a super long ball, it may reach 400. (Some go well over 400 feet.) You can tell its very long if it lands way up in the fans' seats out in the outfield.

Thus, if you see the ball go twenty or thirty rows up into the seats, you can safely guess it is near 400 feet. Your statement then will be accurate.

But notice the look on your man's face when you say that after a home run. It will be amazement, delight, and pride. He'll be thinking what good judgment you have to be able to estimate the distance of a home run ball.

He may not agree with you, and he may say something like, "Naw, couldn't be more than 380." Okay, that's fine. Just say, "Think so?" This is great. He's really talking baseball with you in that case. (Not to you, but with you.) Break through.

4. I BELIEVE THE UMP MISSED THAT ONE, IT LOOKED OUTSIDE. That means the pitched ball did not go over the home plate where it must be to be in the "strike zone," but it appeared to you to be at the side of the plate, the side away from the batter.

Watch carefully, be sure it is where you think it is. You don't want to say it's outside if it is inside. Watch closely.

## HOW TO CATCH—AND KEEP—A MAN
*(How to Love an American Man)*

This is another case where you will want to watch very critically for awhile to be sure you can tell where the ball passes over the plate into the hands of the catcher.

Your man will be looking, also, and he'll have his opinion about the pitch, but it's okay if you see it one way and he sees it another. It's kind of a judgment call, and he knows you could be right. It's a matter of inches.

When you believe you can tell where the ball goes across the plate, speak up.

5. THE CATCHER PUT THAT BALL RIGHT ON SECOND BASE. One of the prettiest plays in baseball is when the catcher throws the ball to second base when a runner is trying to "steal" second from first base. If he throws it in time for the infielder to put the ball on the runner before he gets his foot on the base, the runner is out. If the runner beats the "tag," he's safe.

The more accurate, quick, and strong the catcher, the fewer times a runner is able to steal on him. The key thing is for the catcher to throw the ball to the side of second base that faces first base and down low so the infielder catches the ball a few inches off the ground so the runner's foot is touched with the glove (or ball) when the ball is in the glove. If this "tag" is made, the catcher is said to have "put the ball right on second base."

*Donald Petty*

    This is surely a good observation for you to make when watching the game with your man. He'll be very pleased with your knowing the key is the arm of the catcher.

    6. LOOKED LIKE HE MIGHT HAVE BEAT THAT ONE OUT. This refers to a play at first base when the ball gets to the first baseman almost at the exact same time the runner (who just batted the ball on the ground) gets there.

    The faster the batter, the more likely he is to "beat out" a ground ball or "bunt." The umpire's word is what determines the results of the play.

    The umpire determines which gets to the base first—ball or runner—by comparing what he sees with what he hears. He will watch the foot of the runner step on the base and listen for the ball to hit into the first baseman's glove or vice versa. In that way, he is not caught with his eyes in the wrong place and miss the call.

    If the play is close, it looks different sometimes than what the umpire sees and hears. This is a call the umpire seldom misses; but it still is impressive to the American man for you to think the runner might have

*HOW TO CATCH—AND KEEP—A MAN*
*(How to Love an American Man)*

"beat out" a hit when the umpire calls him out. He is happy you're into the game that deeply.

7. THINK OF HOW DIFFERENT THE GAME WOULD BE IF THE BASE PATHS WERE ONLY EIGHTY-SEVEN FEET. This question-comment would be a terrific thought-provoker for many men. Since there are many close plays in baseball, the difference of three feet (eighty-seven versus ninety) would make more base runners, more hits, more scores, more steals, more extra base hits, higher batting averages, fewer pick offs, higher slugging percentages, and no telling what else would change.

At any rate, you could please your baseball fan by asking such a question. It would reveal to him another point of interest that you show in the game and share with him. In addition, just the imaginative question itself might make him see different things about you. Bottom line, as with all these questions, it provides more good communication between you and the man, and on his turf where he can talk more and longer.

He will like your "deeper" insight into the game of baseball when you ask a thought question such as this one.

8. THE OUTFIELDERS USED TO CATCH WITH BOTH HANDS; WHY DO THEY JUST USE ONE NOW? This is an interesting question for anyone, and your man may develop a theory as good as anybody else's. He may come up with things like:

- They have more confidence now.
- They are better now.
- They are allowed to express their confidence now.
- Statistics show a one-hand catch is as successful as a two-hand one.
- More TV so close-ups look "cooler" now.
- It's a fad.
- The gloves are better.

See how much fun this can be along with his seeing how observant you are? This is a fun question you can both enjoy.

The things to say about baseball will help to endear you to your man. You can learn about ball, about him; and he can learn about you and enjoy your interest in a game he likes. These questions should be win situations for both of you.

## CHAPTER TWENTY-FOUR
## SIX THINGS NOT TO SAY ABOUT BASEBALL

> One of the things about equality is not just that you be treated equally to a man, but that you treat yourself equally to the way you treat a man.
>
> Marlo Thomas

If your man is into baseball, one way or another, or to some degree, it will be good for you to understand as much as possible about the game. Therefore, the positive things you learned will be complemented by your ability not to say things about the sport that would belie a basic insensitivity or naivete or just plain simplicity. The sharper you are about this game (and indeed any sport he's interested in), the more interest your man will have in your thoughts and ideas.

The more you discuss the game with him, the more likely he is to express his feelings and emotions to you about this, as well as other things. When you are both opening up to each other about things of mutual interest, the better, and probably longer, the relationship.

Thus, following are things that are not good to say about baseball.

1. HOW MANY INNINGS DO THEY PLAY? The number of innings (or "at bats") the teams have—nine—is basic to the game; and everyone in America really is likely to be able to answer the question correctly. A normal game provides for one team to have a "three-out, at bat" nine times during a game. The opposition (and home team) will also have nine at-bats. Their three outs will come after the visiting team makes three outs.

In the minor leagues, a seven-inning game can be played as one game of a "double header" (two games in one day). If a game reaches four and a half innings, it becomes an official game and will go into the record even if it gets "called" because of rain or lateness or any other game-stopping event.

*HOW TO CATCH—AND KEEP—A MAN*
*(How to Love an American Man)*

Then, there are "extra inning" games that occur when both teams have the same score at the end of nine innings, and the game is continued in order to break the tie.

2. HOW MANY PLAYERS ARE ON A TEAM? Most men will not be able to answer this for a fact, but the question may be taken two ways. First, it normally would mean, "How many players take the field?" That answer is nine. Second, it may mean, "How many total players make up the full roster?" That is the part the man does not usually know. The answer is twenty-five.

In the American League, there are ten players that start a game for each team; while in the National League, there are nine. The reason there is a difference is because of the "designated hitter" (DH) in the American League. He is a batter that hits in place of a pitcher, who necessarily spends all his effort on pitching; and he may be a poor hitter, and some believe he may "strain" something swinging a bat. The DH keeps that from happening.

Additionally, substitutes may be used to replace players all through the game; but once a player comes out of the game, he cannot return to play until the next game.

*Donald Petty*

The number of players playing the game is usually nine (DH's may not always be used) or one for every position (catcher, pitcher, first base, second base, third base, short stop, left field, center field, right field, and DH (in the American League).

3. WHY ARE THERE FOUR BALLS TO WALK, BUT ONLY THREE STRIKES? You are advised not to ask this question because the man does not really know most of the time. He will refer to the relative value of the ball and strike or the ease of pitching a ball versus a strike; but he cannot really tell you to your satisfaction.

Any frustrating question will simply cause him to tell you that it is just a part of the rules of the game.

Now, if you can turn up with the real reason, he would be interested in your "telling" him, if you frame the comment as a question, so as not to show him up.

Recall, four balls to walk, three strikes for an out.

4. DO THEY ALWAYS MAKE THREE OUTS IN AN INNING? "Yes," is the answer, but this is basic and fundamental and too simple to ask. He will not be impressed by this question.

There is an exception, however, when the game is tied in the ninth (or extra) inning, last half, and a score is

*HOW TO CATCH—AND KEEP—A MAN*
*(How to Love an American Man)*

made. The game ends, regardless of how many outs they have.

5. WHY DO THEY HAVE ONLY ONE SHORT STOP; WHY NOT ONE BETWEEN FIRST AND SECOND? Well, on the surface, this sounds like a pretty good question, but all the man is likely to say is that second baseman acts like the short stop.

That doesn't really answer the question because balls are still hit down the middle through the pitcher's box and over second base into center field. If the second baseman stayed at second, that would not happen.

It just comes down to the rules. He will only say that the rules were written that way, and he'll be a little irritated.

6. WHY DO THEY SOMETIMES JUST QUIT IN THE MIDDLE OF THE NINTH INNING? The game goes nine innings, but if the team that bats last in the inning (i.e. during the last or bottom part of the inning) is ahead, and the other team makes three outs, the game ends. It's over. The more than full figure lady has again sung; thus, there is no need for further hitting by the winner.

This question can be answered by the man who may say the winner does not bat again so as not to "run

*Donald Petty*

up the score." Any reason he gives is probably going to be right, but he will not think you should have to ask it. He'll think you should have figured it out on your own without having to ask.

These questions are ones that a man would think should be self-evident; and although he may be able to answer them for you, it will be as though he had rather not be troubled. He had rather you ask more piercing and more incisive ones. He wants to imagine you as a sharp fan...almost as sharp as he is when it comes to ball.

## CHAPTER TWENTY-FIVE

## SIX THINGS TO SAY ABOUT BASKETBALL

Life is so constructed, that the event does not, cannot, will not, match the expectation.

Charlotte Bronte

Basketball is not as popular as football and baseball, but a man can be just as avid a fan for the game as he is other sports. It is an opportunity to build or strengthen bridges between you and him. Any common interest helps love grow and bonds get stronger.

With that in mind, it will be good for you to know something about basketball. The game is played during the cool and cold months like football. It overlaps in the spring with baseball; therefore, you may see a man using his "Flashback" button on the TV remote control a lot. He may flash from football to basketball in the fall and winter and from baseball to basketball in the spring. That turns out to be okay for you, he is enthused; although for your programming during those times you need another TV.

Guys are somewhat selfish anyway, but during serious sports on TV they really do not share TV time well—but you are always welcome to watch with them. It is especially true of basketball, because it is more of a visual action game. You and he can talk more during this game than while the others are going on. The only other "good-talking" game is golf.

Here, then, are some thing to say about basketball.

1. THIS GAME HAS A LOT OF FREE THROWS. That is a good observation. That indicates you have a studied opinion about the game and feel confident to express it. You will also have a high percentage of men that will be on your side; yet, some men live by the free throw (like the point-after in football) and build strategies on it.

The free throw comes after some one has been fouled or a team has done something wrong. Usually it occurs when a player is about to shoot the ball at the

## HOW TO CATCH—AND KEEP—A MAN
### (How to Love an American Man)

basket and an opposing player hits his arm while trying to block the shot by putting his hand on the ball. The official blows the whistle, stops the game, stops the clock, allows the teams to line up just outside the lane; and the fouled player shoots his free throw (or throws, depending upon the foul that was called). This time is very slow, even draggy; and many people wish they would just take the ball from out of bounds when there is an infraction of the rules, to keep the game moving.

After you watch the game for awhile and you understand when the free throws occur, your comment will be well received.

2. NOBODY "SAILED" TO THE BASKET LIKE DR. JAY DID..., UNLESS IT IS JORDAN. Wow! That will be a heavy comment. Always you will need to know what you are talking about in order to speak with sincerity; thus, you should make this comment only after you have seen old footage of Dr. Jay and watched Michael Jordan play.

That way you can compare the two men who both soar unbelievably long and high to "dunk" the ball into the basket. But plan to learn the "anti-gravity" talent of both men and use the line sometime in a Chicago Bull game, when Michael is playing.

3. THE BULLS MUST HAVE BEEN THE STRONGEST DYNASTY EVER. This comment would refer to their winning five out of six championships in the 1990's. Michael Jordan was their star along with Scottie Pippin and strong supporting players. Even Dennis Rodman did a lot for the team in the latter years.

Before these days there were strong Boston Celtic and Los Angeles Lakers teams; but none of them truly dominated like Chicago. No one could hold a candle to them; therefore, your comment would be accurate, plain, and meaningful to a man.

4. HOW MANY FOULS DOES THAT MAKE? This refers again to the game being stopped for foul calls. It seems they play a minute and stop, play one minute and stop.

If the stopping could be eliminated and the game allowed to progress, it would be equally fair for all and the fans would be better entertained. The games could be full fifteen-minute quarters (instead of twelve) and the game would still finish quicker.

The fouls could be called only when they were flagrant; and the offending player should be sat on the bench on his second foul of the game. That way there would be more action and players would stop the flagrant infractions.

If you understand the argument above, state it, and he will think about it a lot and be astonished at you for saying it.

5. WHY ARE THE NUMBER OF TIME-OUTS LIMITED? The fans would get more activity packed closer together, though the teams would need to rest some more often.

There could be five full time outs to allow teams to "catch their breath"; but also more substitutions could rest the starters and spread the success of the team over more players.

Action-oriented comments would spice up the thinking of your man.

6. I BELIEVE BASKETBALL WAS MORE EXCITING WITH "SHOWTIME" IN L.A. "Showtime" refers to the championship Laker teams which included Magic Johnson, Karim Abdul Jabbar, James Worthy and a great team of support players through the mid and late 1980's. Their fast-break style of play caused fans to cheer and stand and "be proud" more than any other team before or since.

*Donald Petty*

It was magic basketball, cliff hanging wins, near-impossible shots, and innovative plays that captured the sports heads of Americans. Some were converted to basketball by "Showtime" in the play offs and world championship play.

As in every case, make your comments from a source of knowledge, confidence, and sincerity. Know about "Showtime" before you wade off into it. When the man hears about "Showtime in L.A." from you, his ears will perk up.

Basketball comments made appropriately during the game will set you in high esteem with your man. Choose the right time to make them so that you blend in to the game flow.

This common ground will again let you build on the relationship.

## CHAPTER TWENTY-SIX
## SIX THINGS NOT TO SAY ABOUT BASKETBALL

*Nobody can make you feel inferior without your consent.*

Eleanor Roosevelt

Certainly the game of basketball excites the man who is a fan, especially during the play offs. Many men have played basketball as a child, but not as many as have played softball, baseball, and football. They will know the game, but not the inside details like the other two sports.

Still there are some things not to say because of what they communicate. It is like other "things of interest" to the man, he likes for you to be a part of his life, mostly as it relates to him or how he defines it.

The wise woman wanting to love a man and seriously wanting him to love her will heed the comments about liking what he likes and talking in terms of his interest. Basketball may be one of his interests.

Here then are some things not to say about basketball.

1. HOW MUCH DOES A BASKET COUNT? One, two, or three? Actually, the answer to the question is, "Yes." Different baskets count different scores. A free throw is one, a shot inside the "three-point ring" is two, and a shot outside the "three-point line" is three. Generally, the question would imply a shot inside the "three-point line" and would be worth two points. Most of the scoring in a game is done from this distance on the court.

If the man answered the question he would say, "two," with the two exceptions cited above. And he would know that you wanted the typical answer; however, he really, down deep will think you should already know that.

2. CAN WHITE MEN REALLY NOT JUMP AS HIGH AS BLACK MEN? No one really knows. If he is white he would not like admitting he can't jump as well. If he is black, he would not want to say it boastfully.

You may ask a white or black man, but most men will try to be diplomatic and not offend anybody. (To the question, your author would simply suggest that white men do not soar.)

3. WHY ARE THERE SO MANY BLACK MEN AND SO FEW WHITE MEN PLAYING? The white man again will have difficulty with this question. The black man will think, "Isn't it self-evident?"

The question does not lend itself to a comfortable answer, and it should not be asked. It does not raise good feelings with the one you are trying to love; therefore, it does not meet your objectives.

4. WHY DO THEY HAVE TWENTY-FOUR SECONDS TO SHOOT, AND NOT TWENTY-FIVE? Well, you will stump your man again with this question because he will not know. As before, your questions need to do three things: give him an opportunity to answer well (to stroke his ego), give you information, and show him you are interested in his things by impressing him with good questions.

This question does not qualify on all three points because he cannot show how much he knows about basketball. It will be a putdown for him and that is counter-productive for your purposes.

5. HOW MANY MEN ARE ON ONE TEAM? Five men per team play at one time, but twelve men make up the team. Generally the man will not know this answer positively; thus, you run the risk of two things occurring to him. First, he will think you should know five are on the court at once. Second, he will be unsure of the total number of team members.

In either case discomfort ensues, and that is not positive for your relationship.

6. WHAT IS A DOUBLE DRIBBLE; FOR THAT MATTER, WHAT IS A DRIBBLE, AND IS THERE A TRIPLE DRIBBLE? Dribbling is bouncing the ball on the floor in a steady rhythm. If the bouncing is stopped (in the mind of the official) and restarted, it is a double dribble, and a penalty is called.

A triple dribble does not happen because a double dribble stops the play and brings a penalty before the third start of bouncing the ball can begin. There is no triple dribble.

The question will be one the man thinks you should know or pick up without asking. He will take time to answer, but he will at the same time think it is too fundamental to talk about.

*HOW TO CATCH—AND KEEP—A MAN*
*(How to Love an American Man)*

These basketball questions not to ask are things you can learn on your own and thus turn them into positive comments with favorable results. As questions, however, they do not enhance the relationship!

## CHAPTER TWENTY-SEVEN
## NINE THINGS TO SAY ABOUT GOLF

What is important to a relationship is a harmony of emotional roles and not too great a disparity in the general level of intelligence.

Mirra Komarovsky

Golf is the game the man plays "to relax." And if you believe that, there is swamp land you may enjoy in Florida. The two reasons the game is played, according to business men across the United States are "to relax" (or unwind) and "to get exercise." True? Neither one.

They do not relax; they compete and rail out and slam clubs into the ground or woods or lake. Their faces turn red, they grimace, their blood pressure rises, they gasp for air, they fudge, they write down a lower number than they shoot, they rationalize, they complain and grumble, they point fingers, they blame the elements, insects, weather (even God!). Does that sound to you like they are relaxing?

They do not get exercise because they ride carts or have someone else carry their clubs or just amble around to keep from getting tired or overworked. They are tense and get stressed out so they are not exercising.

Yet, there are some very good things you may be able to say to your "course warrior" that will lift him up, endear your self to his golf play, and enhance your relationship. Here are some of them for your consideration.

1. IS THE PUTTER ONLY USED ON THE GREEN? At first it seems evident that it is, but on closer view it is seen that pro golfers may use it when the are on the "frog hair" (just off the green) and even in other flat, low grass lies. Thus, your golfing man will appreciate this question and give thought to his answer.

The question will register credence in his mind and pique his consciousness of your interest. Good on these two points plus you learn and the two of you communicate more. Good.

*HOW TO CATCH—AND KEEP—A MAN*
*(How to Love an American Man)*

2. HOW MANY WOODS ARE THERE? He will count driver, one, two, three, four, and probably volunteer the ways and places and times they are used.

Woods are used for long shots off the tee and on the fairways. Generally the longer the shot the lower the number. Following the wood shots are the iron shots, then comes the putter to aim for the hole.

All in all, this is a good question. He will have a good idea of what to answer and will take time to explain, as this is a good question.

3. CAN THE LONGEST IRON BE USED IN PLACE OF A WOOD? WHEN? Yes, in some cases. He really may not know the best answer here, but he knows he has done it and has seen the pros do it. Good piercing questions like this one, though, show real interest in the game. You win regardless of the answer.

The answer to the "When?" part is actually, "when course position says a wood might provide too much distance."

4. ARE SEVENTY-TWO HOLES ALWAYS PLAYED IN A PGA TOURNAMENT? While your man may not always know the answer to this one, he will answer something like, "As far as I know," or "I believe so." He'll be right. They try to play 18 holes on each of four days,

*Donald Petty*

Thursday through Sunday. They normally "qualify" on Wednesday before the tournament.

When the PGA tournaments have the most exciting rounds on Saturday and Sunday, more people watch on TV, (making the advertising bucks a whole lot bigger!). A nice question like this one gives him a nice feeling, he can understand and answer intelligently and you look good. Ask it.

5. IS PAR THE SAME FOR PROS AS AMATEURS? Good question. Most men will say "yes." The pros will reach or break par far more often than the amateur; but the hole has a par value based on physics. How far does the ball go when hit with a certain force? How long are the fairways? How difficult are the obstacles? What kinds of turns, hills, fairway grass? How large is the green? Where is the cup placement? All This is mathematically determined.

One man (or woman) has as much chance to practice as another; therefore, par is par...for men. For women all the same rules apply except par is slightly higher for women than it is for men.

These numbers are based on averages of players. Good question; listen for his fun answer.

6. WHAT DETERMINES THE "PAR" OF A HOLE? WHO DOES IT? The number five question above led to the answer to this first part. The second part deserves an answer, but your man may fumble around a bit with that answer. He'll wind up concluding it is a committee of the Professional Golfer Association (PGA) which approves par.

What he may not know is that the owner-designer-builder sets par when the course is created.

The designer's judgement is based on experience, testing, application of rules for par, and observing the play to confirm that in practice it is what they envisioned.

7. HOW DO THEY DETERMINE THE "CUT" FOR A TOURNAMENT? The cut comes on Wednesday before tournament play begins on Thursday. The number of players that score the best (lowest) round on Wednesday get to play in the tournament.

The tournament rules state how many players will play; therefore, the number of entrants who score best on Wednesday play the tournament.

8. HOW DO THEY DETERMINE HOW MUCH MONEY GOES TO THE WINNER? It's a percentage of purse formula based on past experiences but firm when

the tournament is announced. The tournament authorities know what to expect in revenues (from the gate and TV); thus, they know what they can offer to draw the best crowds and coverage.

Once the award money is announced it is not revoked regardless of the income from the tournament.

9. ARE THEY RESTRICTED TO A CERTAIN TYPE GOLF BALL? The PGA has golf ball requirements and tests for those requirements. Any ball used in the tournament must meet the standards. Everyone entering the tournament knows which balls meet or fail the standards.

All manufacturers of golf balls selling them for tournament play have rigid specifications and accurate tests to guarantee conformity.

Some cheaper balls made for the amateur do not have to meet specs.

Ask questions about golf that are insightful, answerable, but challenging. They will make your relationship better and stronger. He may even want to buy you a set of clubs.

Enjoy asking and hearing his answer.

## CHAPTER TWENTY-EIGHT
## FIVE THINGS NOT TO SAY ABOUT GOLF

> For a certain type of woman who risks losing her identity in a man, there are all those questions...until you get to the point and know that you really are living a love story.
>
> Anouk Aimée

Golf seems to be a rather simple game, and many men know quite a lot about it. Yet it has some extremely technical aspects that require skill and practice to master.

The very simple parts of the game can be deceiving if taken too lightly. No component of the game should be overlooked, and surely any question you ask should be

Donald Petty

considered before it rolls off your tongue. Your questions are a powerful source for the good of your relationship or a strong force for damage to your relationship. Weigh them before you ask them.

This chapter discusses some things you had best leave unasked.

1. WHY DON'T THEY BUILD THE COURSE FURTHER AWAY FROM THE WATER? Challenges built into the game add interest to the play. It is one thing to nudge your ball a little with your foot when you're behind a tree; but remove the water? No way, never! It could be considered sacrilege and you may not be forgiven.

The man has to be able to work around or over the water to be a man of golf.

2. WHY ALL THAT SAND NEAR THE GREEN? The sand trap is another form of challenge. It's a challenge to blast out of trap (preferably on film, or at least with credible witnesses).

Grass in the sand trap (bunker)! Burn his house first. Steal his car. Cut off his little finger, but never consider asking that question.

3. WHY DO THEY JERK THE TV CAMERAS FROM HOLE TO HOLE? Who can keep up? The avid male golf

fan can keep up, but your author is with you. The man will not tolerate your changing the game, TV coverage, or commercials. The camera man will watch the swings of importance, whatever hole they are playing, and the viewer usually agrees.

4. WHAT DO THE OFFICIALS DO, HOW MANY ARE THERE, AND WHAT ARE THEY CALLED? The officials make rulings on where the ball "lies"; they ensure correct scoring, see that the ball is not illegally touched and determine if score cards are properly signed.

5. ISN'T THERE REALLY SOMETHING MORE IMPORTANT FOR PEOPLE TO DO THAN TRY TO PUT THE BALL IN THE CUP? Unless you are ready to truly sign away this part of his life and the opportunity to share many hours of golf talk this question must be buried to never be raised. This is a death knell to a great potential segment of life with your golfing male.

All this chapter has been for is to give you an idea of the type of things not to say regarding the game of golf. Your golfing man will spend hours in his lifetime talking about shots he has made.

Avoid allowing yourself to say anything about golf that puts you in a bad light.

## CHAPTER TWENTY-NINE
## EIGHT THINGS TO SAY ABOUT OTHER FEMALES

>No partner in a love relationship...should feel that he has to give up an essential part of himself to make it viable.
>
>May Sarton

No doubt about it, a man likes to talk about females. He talks about them to other men as often as he holds a conversation; and he talks to females as often as possible. But, this is a mine field like none other for you. You can blow up a relationship easily in this territory.

Being very careful to remain as neutral in emotion and inflection as you can be, the following samples of things to say about other women may be helpful as you are developing your relationship with a man.

1. SHE IS NICE. He will agree, but keep in mind, it is a mine field for him, too. He also can blow it! If you say they are "nice," he will agree, but he cannot agree vociferously. He has only to say, "Yes, some of them."

If he says, "Wow, I know!" he has upset you. If he says, "No, I disagree," he is not being truthful plus he strikes a cord of disagreement with you. He doesn't want to do that either. Thus, he's on a fine wire along with you.

Your admitting some of the other girls are "nice" puts you on his side and lets him see you are not going into a jealous or possessive attitude—both are good.

At the same time, it is not a good idea to be too complimentary about any one girl or especially any specific trait that you do not have. If you have beautiful hair, comment how "nice" the other woman's hair looks. If your teeth are fantastic, talk about the other girl's "nice" teeth. If you have gorgeous eyes, say how "nice" the other female's eyes are.

2. SHE REALLY KNOWS HOW TO DRESS. This is a good comment as long as you know how to dress and

do so. If you dress very well, you of course can say she dresses "nicely." Do not search for words.

When you comment on another woman, you do not want it to sound icy or derogatory. The last thing you need is for him to think you lack confidence; therefore, there should be no reason to stoop to criticizing others.

3. SHE SELECTS NICE FRAGRANCES. This again shows you have confidence and that you are attuned to the perfumes that are being used. You, naturally, need to be wearing the right one for you...and know it.

Any comments you make should be sincere and from a true store of knowledge, not just light or simple or made up. If your relationship, indeed your life, is being prepared for in your comments, isn't it wise to study up and know that about which you speak?

Know about fragrances and be aware of the value of them. Knowing perfumes is for appropriate use, not for snobbery or attacking another woman.

4. SHE HAS NICE HAIR. You have learned by now you are well advised to make nice remarks about other women. He has noticed them, whether he tries to act like he has or not. If he is not dumb, blind, or insensitive; he will notice other women's hair. But he's with you by choice, his as well as yours. He may have

already noticed your hair. If so, it may have elicited a compliment by now.

It is good for you to feel comfortable making positive statements about other women. Do it.

5. SHE IS NATURALLY ATTRACTIVE. This is a statement that will conjure up in his mind some of the "natural" features you want him to see in you. It will work; he will immediately see beauty in you and most likely say it.

These words are so normal and true and accurate that he will enjoy thinking about them with you. "Naturally attractive." Yes, he may enjoy telling you about your natural beauty.

The door you open for him in these compliments about other women gives him many things to say about you that are delicious. He'll be thankful for the opportunity to speak about the naturalness and the beauty of the woman he is with, you may not need to say anything further.

6. SHE REALLY KNOWS HOW TO ORGANIZE THEIR LIVES. Yes, say this, but not in a negative way that indicates that you do not know how to be organized. If you call attention to the ability to organize, you may be letting him know you are an organized woman yourself.

It is not a productive tact to beg a compliment by claiming a weakness. There is no need to make a flimsy statement like, "I wish I were organized," just to cause him to say, "But you are!" Just be organized; he'll recognize it!

7. SHE MUST MAKE AN INTERESTING DATE. This is a question that will cause a man to talk about what constitutes an interesting date as he sees it. This will give you an opportunity to learn a lot about what he thinks about going out and how to treat a woman.

Is he fun, adventurous, generous, tight, bawdy, conservative, serious? His ideas on dating and interesting dates will help answer those questions.

Follow-up questions should be interesting for both of you. Just let it flow.

8. SHE IS A GOOD EMPLOYEE. This one is a little touchy, since he may have some preconceived ideas about some particular woman in the workplace either from stereotypical impressions, jokes, or in some instances, personal experiences. This is not one to push to a defense-offense level.

If he is pretty positive about it, let it move along; but if he seems uncomfortable or defensive or even hostile and aggressive, get off it. Change the subject. He may not be openly understanding of females he works with, even though he may try to accept and see the right things. Allow him room and time to fidget, and be understanding yourself if a great deal of "role confusion" exists in him.

This chapter has been written to give you a range of ideas to talk about in regard to other women. Notice nothing was said about asking him specifically about his other women past (or present). Only generalizations about "other" women are advised. No woman in particular should be singled out, as it gets personal and appears to him as meddling or even worse, needling. If you are building a relationship, needling is not a good part of the mix.

## CHAPTER THIRTY
## TEN THINGS NOT TO SAY ABOUT OTHER FEMALES

> I was at a party feeling very shy because there were a lot of celebrities around, and I was sitting in a corner alone and a very beautiful young man came up to me and offered me some salted peanuts and he said, "I wish they were emeralds" as he handed me the peanuts and that was the end of my heart. I never got it back.
>
> Helen Hayes

You can tear up or set back a strong and growing relationship by saying the exact wrong thing to a man. He may sense in you some anti-male words, and it may

*Donald Petty*

give him second thoughts about spending a lifetime with you.

He may hear crusade, feminist, bashing, threatened, intimidated, discrimination, equal rights, and such like. These are words that may have caused him heartaches, headaches, confusion, disruption, disappointment; and they may have cost him promotions, positions, jobs, income, recognition.

The point is not whether these things are right or not; rather, it is that he may have these perceptions, true or not. He may not be sure what has happened to his world, and he may believe he sees a lot of mistakes being made and things going in the wrong direction.

It is not something that is likely to change in his mind any time soon; thus, the recommendation of things not to say to him are included here for your careful consideration.

1. WOMEN GENERALLY GET A JOB DONE BETTER THAN A MAN. Many things have been written, and jokes told, and sitcoms have portrayed women doing a lot of things better than men. In fact, many TV shows characterize fathers as oafs and butts of jokes. All this goes to cause some men to feel belittled and offended. He does not feel like a dummy, but these shows make

him appear unable to do things; then a woman appears and makes the task look easy.

Certainly there are occasions where women do things better than men, and vice versa. The problem with the comment is the word "generally." If it were "sometimes," the edge of the thought would be removed, but as it stands, an insecure man would not appreciate the statement, and your relationship would suffer a setback if you said it.

2. WOMEN CANNOT GET A JOB DONE AS WELL AS MEN. This comment is about equal to number one. A man does not want to hear a woman (or women) put down in that way. In some cases, a man can do a job better than women, and vice versa.

You will have a happier man if you do not put down either men or women.

3. WOMEN ARE EQUAL TO MEN, JUST DIFFERENT. There are enough differences in a man and a woman to make it seem obvious that the statement has to be explained and redefined.

Plainly, many women in many areas are significantly superior, and vice versa. Thus, when equality is declared, there must be more explanation or the man does not agree. Not a choice comment to make by a woman seeking to keep a man.

4. MORE WOMEN SHOULD BE CEOs AND PRESIDENTS. A man would not have a problem with qualified women rising to the top of their companies. But to just make the blanket statement would be to beg an issue with him. If the comment were more on the order of, "More women should figure out the way to earn the level of CEO or president," he would support the contention.

Many men do not believe women are natural leaders or destined administrators of companies (or countries), but they may accept a woman leader who has earned her way to the top.

Again, it is a matter of semantics. If the woman's belief is that a woman to rise in her organization must do it by competing equally with other employees, a man will support her.

5. ONE DAY A WOMAN WILL BE PRESIDENT. Okay. That is okay. If there is a woman who has stated her views and agenda, convinced a majority of voters that she can run the country, and has done work to prove she is capable of the office, she can probably count on job.

In this situation, as with the previous ones, the woman's traits, character, record, and potential far outweigh her gender characteristics in the mind of the voting male. The statement should be framed in that light rather than a prophesy of determination and crusade.

6. I ADMIRE FEMINIST LEADERS. Most men will not share your admiration. They may understand your desire for (and right to) equal rights, and may understand the movement and the fight. But most do not condone the pulling down of men by the words of women, nor will they grasp the strategy of bashing men. Those type things done by feminists and their followers (and dupes) are negatives and will not enhance the relationship you are striving to nourish.

7. WOMEN IN COMBAT CARRY THEIR LOAD. Many men in combat have not yet agreed with that; although as yet the real tests have not been given. Since the Crimean War, women have carried out their assignments well.

The man you are trying to love may not be excited about a comment on the prowess of a woman in combat. It may be hard for him to imagine a woman "manning" a 30-caliber machine gun from atop a burning tank and killing over 200 of the enemy. The image may not clearly come into focus for him.

8. SOME WOMEN UNDERSTAND MEN BETTER THAN SOME MEN UNDERSTAND WOMEN. A man will usually agree that men do not understand women, but in truth, he has reached the point where most believe women do not understand men any better. However, the thinking man will defy those definitions and deny a belief that a woman knows much about him at all.

Much of the time, she does not know what he really thinks about. She cannot always know what hurts him. She has little way of knowing his emotions when he is rejected or made fun of or ignored or praised or tricked or manipulated or passed over, or when he hits a home run or a three-shot basket or makes a T.D.

Best again to lay off the comment unless you can have a sit-com in mind where both of you can laugh.

9. WOMEN ARE MORE SENSITIVE THAN MEN. It does not seem within the purvey of a woman to know enough about the sensitivity of a man to be able to make the statement. He may not even know why she would say that because he recounts the times when his love overflowed in his heart, when he watched her work or

play or worship, and he had a great welling up of feelings.

He may not think he is insensitive; and he wonders how she could feel sensitive when she "bawls him out" or "barks" commands or heaps ridicule. How can he feel agreeable about the comment?

10. THERE ARE A LOT OF WOMEN OUT THERE YOU COULD DATE; WHY DID YOU ASK ME OUT? The question is not a good one because it belittles you. He wonders, "What is wrong with you that I should not date you" In addition, it would come across to him that you do not think highly of yourself. He would not see it as a question of interest, but as one of wonder and amazement. "Why in the world would a man go with me?!"

Worst of all possibilities, the man may see the question as a "compliment-seeker." This would give him a feeling that you were not sincerely asking and that you lacked esteem by even wondering about the reasons he asked you out.

This has been a fun chapter for your author and hopefully for you. But more than fun, there were fairly intense philosophical concepts for your consideration and learning. The man inside is not what Hollywood

*Donald Petty*

depicts him as being. He is not all of what the "women's movements" have made him out to be.

Although he should resent being stereotyped, he mostly ignores it or is unaware of it. A great approach to building a true relationship is to avoid the confrontational comments about the gender gap, male-female interfaces, and equality of women. This would be true even within a marriage.

## CHAPTER THIRTY-ONE
## FIVE THINGS TO SAY ABOUT OTHER MALES

> When two people love each other, they don't look at each other, they look in the same direction.
>
> Ginger Rogers

One trend of the last four decades has been to undermine the accomplishments of men and to talk about their shortcomings, insensitivity to women, dishonesty, criminal tendencies, and overall "worthlessness." If you want to build a solid relationship with a man, you will do well to consider and talk about his positive contributions.

Men get tired of hearing how bad they are, whose fault all evil is, and what wrongs men have done. Be ready to give some balance on the positive side. He has done good; he may (or may not) be quiet about it, but inside he wants to know he has done some things right.

You will do well and learn to love and be loved if you will "accentuate the positive, eliminate the negative, latch on to the affirmative," as the old song goes.

1. THERE ARE SOME VERY GOOD MEN IN THIS WORLD. When you say that, you need to be prepared to name some (no jokes here). Seriously, point out the success and achievements and good things men have done. There will be some nice things you will discover as you do your homework here.

It should be natural to point out the good in people in general and men in particular; but you will solidify much about your relationship by pouring on recognition for man's accomplishments instead of his weaknesses.

2. MEN HAVE WORKED HARD TO LIGHTEN THE BURDEN OF WOMEN. Many men have done grand, good, and heroic deeds; many made advances in business and technology, and have invented multitudes of labor-saving devices and machines for production and housework. Most of the things made to save labor in homes have been created because a man watched his mother or spouse or sister do the dishes, wash clothes,

iron, mop, sweep, hang out/bring in the wash, cook, and countless other hot, hard chores.

Because he saw the hardship on the woman, he wanted to relieve as much of it as he could. Washing machines, dish washers, vacuums, dryers, coffeemakers, microwaves, etc. et. al., ad infinitum, were developed to give women more free time to enjoy life and family and her own space and time.

With those thoughts in mind, it should seem to be the woman trying to know how to catch and keep a man and receive his love in return should state that he has done a lot for which gratitude and thanks would be in order. Let him know that you recognize life is better because of men, and say thank you.

3. GREAT MEN HAVE BUILT OUR COUNTRY. Not discounting the contributions by women down through the ages, men have been out front on the line in the trenches fighting, working, hunting, farming, building, doing; while women have provided backup, support, homes, training for kids, household management, and contributed to the workforce.

He will take pride, agree with you, try to do more, and love you for recognizing the contributions made by all.

Donald Petty

4. TOUGH MEN HAVE FOUGHT TO PRESERVE FREEDOM. If that is not the whole story (and it is not), it is a good part of it, and the man's chest will noticeably expand as he hears you say it. Now just here, he is not expecting you to "admit" it (or anything), just say it.

Fighting for territory, homeland, family, possessions is extremely important to most men. Principles and ideas and philosophy are one thing; preserving land, boundaries, and the freedom to live life fully and freely is dear to most men's hearts. Many men will lay down their lives for their women, family, and home.

Make the statement and watch him grow.

5. MEN HAVE FURTHERED SCIENCE, RELIGION, POLITICS, BUSINESS, INDUSTRY, AND EDUCATION. For you to say these things and your man hear them will let him know you are open enough with him to say them with confidence in your own abilities. This phrase is a winner as you do your part to build the relationship. He will respond; he will build much more than his "half" of the partnership. When he knows that you have great feelings for "male-dom" and him, you and he will face a lot more together as a team and in unity.

*HOW TO CATCH—AND KEEP—A MAN*
*(How to Love an American Man)*

Wise women through centuries have known how to compliment men. Wise women of this day still know how. It is unfortunate that the not-so-wise have forgotten the art and principles of praise (not flattery, and never false commendation).

Men have done a lot; women see it and know it; wise ones say it to the men. Her reward comes in the form of her man committing absolutely to her best welfare, her feelings, her complete actualization in life. Say it, and say it a lot.

## CHAPTER THIRTY-TWO
## FIFTEEN THINGS NOT TO SAY ABOUT OTHER MEN

>       True feeling justifies whatever it may cost.
>
>                              May Sarton

Contrary to popular stereotype, the feelings of any man can be touched, even hurt, by the things a woman may say. He may respond with anger or accusation, but the emotion in reality is sensitivity to criticism.

There are critical remarks intended to hurt and others expected to help. Either one may be taken by the man as an accusation that he is deficient in one way or another. This chapter deals with quite a few different types of comments that should not be made if you are partner-making.

You will harm the chances you have of loving a man if you say the wrong things. Here then are some sample statements not to make about other men.

1. HE IS THE BEST LOOKING MAN I EVER SAW. This statement may be true and it can be sincere, but it does not endear your man to you if you say it to him. He likely knows you see other men as handsome, better looking then he is; but he would not know what you meant by saying it. If you want him to be better looking, making this comment will not bring it about.

There should definitely be no reason for you to tell him that he is the best looking man you ever saw if it is not true. It obviously leaves you with the option to not say anybody is the best looking man you ever saw. That is the choice you should make. Say nothing about good looks (unless it might be, "I like your looks").

2. HE IS VERY SENSITIVE WHEN IT COMES TO WOMEN. A man may have two thoughts if you say this. First, how would you know? Second, am I not? Neither thought helps you learn to love him, and vice versa.

There are so many good things to say that lifts his esteem that you should never gamble on something that would put him down, making him self-conscious or doubtful of himself.

Avoid giving any impression that he lacks sensitivity. "Why can't you be like John?" or some such question would hit him hard.

When he does show sensitivity, let him know how much you like it and the degree of appreciation you have for him for sharing. Call it positive re-enforcement and take every opportunity to use it.

3. I LIKE HIS BODY. "So does that mean I'm chopped liver?" You have to be careful how you make specific comments about other men to keep him from being bothered or even a bit jealous or wary.

A man may instantly compares himself with your descriptions of any other man. He sees hidden messages in your compliments of anyone else. He may be egotistical enough (or insecure enough) to think your every comment is in some way directed to him and is about him.

Because of that, when you say, "I like his body," he thinks you mean you are implying that the other guy's body is better than his. Do not chance it.

4. HE IS SO COMPASSIONATE. "How would you know? Why would he show compassion around you?

What has he to be compassionate about when it comes to you? Is he more compassionate than I am? Am I not compassionate? What in the world is compassionate? What do I need to be compassionate about? Is she telling me something? Is she putting me down? Have I missed something? Have I failed to be compassionate? Am I compassionate? What do I need to change to show her I am compassionate?

Can you imagine that flurry of doubt and questions in the mind of a man when you make that simple comment? Unless you know what all will run through his mind, it is best not to make the comment.

5. HE REALLY KNOWS HOW TO TREAT A WOMAN. If you say that, you will put your man into a tail spin trying to figure out what it means and what you think about him. He will wonder if you are unhappy with the way he treats you, and it will not make him treat you any differently; it will only make him question your definition of "good treatment" and his own ability and skill at treating you right.

(NOTE: You command respect and good treatment by your actions, not by demanding it verbally.)

6. I'D LIKE TO GO OUT WITH HIM. If this is intended to make a man respect you or like you more or

treat you differently, you will be disappointed. His first reaction will be, "Well, go with him if you'd like to," and he will mean it.

This comment is a relationship buster. Say it only when you do not care if the relationship is over. If you really mean it, do as you will. If it is a teaser, withhold it.

7. I LIKE MEN WHO TREAT ME LIKE A WOMAN. A man wants you to be that way and feel that way, but he had rather you not say it to him about himself or about anyone else. Most men like, and come to love, feminine women. Do not mistake the word feminine with weakness. He is not looking for a weak woman; rather, he is hoping to live his life with a very exciting woman confident of her femininity.

A woman who is comfortable with herself as a total woman can make a man feel and act like a complete masculine man. That is his role and he wants to live his life that way; thus, he can be totally content for life with a woman exercising her rights and living her life with the traits, words, actions, and thoughts as a woman.

It is not to be said; it is to be lived, and you will command treatment as a woman.

8. HE REALLY SPENDS MONEY ON HIS DATES. The words money and dates need not, indeed should not,

be connected. The money he spends is not what he tries to do (or not do). What he wants to do are things he believes you will enjoy, remember, want to repeat, judge him by, and learn to like him because he does them, not because he spends a lot of money doing them.

The phrase can be bad because he thinks (1) you are judging him by how much he spends, (2) you are interested in his money, or (3) you are encouraging him (or asking him) to spend money on you. It's like asking for a gift. Do not do it.

9. HE DRIVES A REALLY FINE CAR. This comment can make a man think cars (wealth or prestige) are too important to you. He really does not want to be judged by his money, car, clothes, or any "material" possessions. He wants to be seen and dated (and loved) because of his personality and judgment (wisdom) and wit.

Even the statement, "I like your car," can indicate your assessment of his financial status; be careful in any comment about cars. Perhaps you could say something like, "Tell me about your car." Then, you let him talk, without judging. In addition, you'll learn a bit about his likes and dislikes and concerns.

10. HE IS ON A FAST TRACK IN HIS COMPANY. "And I'm not! And I'm not?" either phrase of which the man will/could think. It sounds to him as though you could be worried about his career, your security, or prestige.

Any time he feels "measured" by your words, he can be made uncomfortable, unconfident, untrusted, or unliked. Better to say things positive about his track or career. You have already learned about his job, his attitude about his job, and where he is going. If you still are interested in him and his earning power (not only "potential"), you need not worry about it or talk about it anymore.

11. HE REALLY WORKS AROUND THE YARD. If you like the way his yard looks, you should say so. "Your yard always looks fine." He'll know how he got it that way and the comment helps him to continue working that way.

If he thinks you just want him to sweat in the yard with hard work to keep up appearance, he can imagine you nagging or gouging him to "cut the grass." He likes results and he prefers your recognizing results rather than the action itself. He does not need a yard supervisor at home or at his place.

12.  HE'S A GREAT COOK.  This sounds like flattery to keep him in the kitchen and you out of the kitchen.  This is between you and him, who cooks if only one of you or both; but he does not want to feel manipulated into cooking by your words of praise.

The average man is not prone to cook or be good baby bathers or diaper changers.  He will when the chips are down; he will do them all when required; but you must be careful not to demand it of him.  Let him see the need; then, he will do it.

If you are sick or overworked or overly stressed, he will lend a hand; but normally speaking, the average man looks for his woman to do the kitchen and childcare things.  He still has the "hunters" instinct, while he sees the woman as the "skinner."  He does not see all chores as 50-50.  He may still feel he has man's chores and you have woman's chores.

He will "give in" to gain your good favor on occasion; but his instincts may still be very much based on male-female jobs.  If he sees cooking as female, he'll see taking you out to eat as male.

13.  HE IS A GREAT HANDYMAN.  He knows sometimes women say this kind of thing, which is like the "works around the yard" comment, to get men to "live

up" to her word and expression of praise. If he senses that the statement is flattery or insincere or manipulative, he may abandon his role as handyman for the most part. He is what he is. He is not a "handyman" if he fixes something and it has to be re-fixed or "over-fixed" by someone else every time.

He may or may not be a fixer-upper. If he really lacks ability or desire, passion or need, he may mess up more than he fixes up, whatever size the job. This will cost more sometimes to undo/redo than if it is done right to begin with.

"He is a great handyman" (spoken about another man or spoken about your man in his presence), is a statement fraught with peril.

14. HE KNOWS JUST WHAT I LIKE. "How?" The man will certainly want to know. This would be a blunder for you to say. The really truthful question naturally and certainly follows, how does he know?

Whether you can answer the question openly and truthfully or not is unimportant. Your man will feel as if he is being compared again; therefore, leave off the comment.

15. SOME MEN UNDERSTAND WOMEN AND SOME DON'T. This one you might get away with if you

attach quickly the following clause. "And you certainly do." But it would be better received by your man if you just make it positive and direct and non-comparative. "You surely do understand me."

But, even then, he may still think there is something hidden you want him to know or that you want him to ask or that you want to say to him but haven't figured out how to do it.

This chapter has presented "cautions" and "red flags" and "absolutely forbidden things" about comments to an American man. Are you realizing how simple, yet complicated, the man can be? How fragile his ego and how easily you smash his feelings and chip away at his confidence?

He wants to put stock in what you say to him; but he can quickly become a skeptic and cynic. You best build him up sincerely, leaving off flattery and criticism (even positive). He does not like to be compared with other men.

He prefers being the only man, the only thing of importance to you when you and he are together. You are wise to be extremely careful what you say to him and how you say things if you want him to be all his nature will allow him to be.

# CHAPTER THIRTY-THREE
# TWENTY-SEVEN FOUR-WORD PHRASES TO AVOID

## IN COMMUNICATING

I don't need an overpowering, powerful, rich man to feel secure. I'd much rather have a man who is there for me, who really loves me, who is growing, who is real.

Bianca Jagger

You may hear about four-letter words that are taboo; in fact, some of them are considered "adult language" when some adults would not even say them. But there are some four-word phrases that should not be spoken to a man you are trying to learn to love. They will set back your progress if he takes them wrong, or in some cases if he takes them "right" (the way you meant him to take them).

1. THAT'S WHAT YOU THINK!  When in discussion with him, and he says something that he believes, this is an improper retort.  If you do not think he is right, it will be better for your argument and your relationship if you say, "Ummm.  I see.  If that is your point of view, I'll try and understand; but with the facts I have now, I do not agree."  And say it as open-mindedly as you can.

2. YES, BUT REMEMBER WHEN...If this is going to dig up some old problem that has been laid to rest in the past, do not say it.  Address only the issue at hand.

3. MY MOTHER ALWAYS SAID...First, that phrase does not automatically make it right.  If it is right, the man is likely turned off by quoting a family member, particular the mother if you're trying to add credibility to your point of view.  (Even if he likes your mom).  He wants your independent opinion.

4. FOR CRYING OUT LOUD!  If you say this in disgust to your man, he will likely feel as though you think he is incapable of rational thought.  It shows you are exasperated, and he then feels you are on separate levels of talk.

5. JUST TELL ME WHY!...This may follow a comment he's made about where he is going or what he will be doing. He will not be moved to tell you "why," not feeling obligated. When you make a demand like this, he will resist a straight answer.

6. TELL ME WHY NOT!...This is kind of like the above. He feels no compulsion to explain himself. Had he wanted to explain it, he would have before you asked him to do so.

7. BUT YESTERDAY YOU SAID...He said what he said yesterday because that's what he knew to say. Today it may be different, and he has changed his statement. It would be a mistake to try to hold him to the words you perceived (or truly heard) if the new day has brought new facts to him.

8. OKAY, BUT MY HEAD HURTS. If this seems like more than four words to you, leave off the "Okay." This would be a complaint or a reason. If it is a reason, just avoid saying, "Okay," and do not do it.

9. DO YOU LIKE KIDS? Loaded or not, this one could make your man run for cover. He reads many possibilities into this question—think about it.

10. WHERE ARE YOU GOING? Not necessary for you to know. But remember, the sword cuts both ways;

he does not always need to know where you are going either. Perhaps you might ask, "Shall I plan lunch at noon?" or some such.

11. PLEASE CUT THE GRASS. He most likely noticed the grass was high and does not have to be told to cut it. Maybe he is not as tidy as you; so if it becomes too much, ask him to show you how to use the mower. If you happen to be cutting it through supper time, it would be tough on him, huh? (Author's opinion? He should cut the grass.)

12. TURN THE THERMOSTAT UP. Uh oh. Two different body temperatures...trouble ahead. If he is hot and you say, "Turn it up," how about his comfort? What about putting on a little warmer clothes? If he is cold and you are warm, ask him if you could bring him a sweater. The premise is that it is easier to get warm than to get cool.

13. I LIVE HERE, TOO. Would that really be news? Does he actually not know that? Better to say something like, "Since we do share our home, would it make sense to compromise and agree that...so and so?"

14. MY CLOTHES ARE RAGS. Exaggeration will not be connected to pity in this case in the mind of the man. He will not be shamed into your point of view. If

you honestly need clothes, buy what you need (operative word "need," not want). If your arrangement is to discuss clothes purchases, do so. But "rags"?! Not believable.

15. DID YOU GET PAID? He senses this as a nagging question. He prefers not being nagged. If you want to learn to love him, it is not good to show concern over his pay.

16. WE NEVER GO OUT. If true, he has to be making a mistake; but how did the relationship get to this point? If it's for a walk or to a cafe, go out. Let him know what fun it is to go out. Figure out inexpensive ways to go out to places he likes also. Ask him to go out, but the comment, "We never go out," sounds immature.

17. YOU KEEP THE KIDS. He will and should some (for the good of all); but demanding it will not be the way to solidify the love-building you have been doing. Many men are usually not as good at keeping kids as a woman. If this is the case, he and the kids know that; thus, "dropping" them on him makes for a bad show. Plan it with him; help him make the time he has them a successful time.

18. YOU DO THE CLOTHES. Many men see the clothes washer being a woman. He may not do a very

good job of washing, folding, or ironing. If he expects this to be a part of your agenda, arrangements may be agreed upon, but demanding that he do the clothes (or anything else) is not a good four-letter phrase.

19. I AM NEVER ALONE. This is an understandable need, but perhaps approaching it in a more positive way would make a better impression and get quicker results. "I need a little time to relax my mind and relieve my emotions." Then discuss some ideas that will give you that time. Have several options so he will see what you really need, and he'll likely help make free time available to you without the sound of a complaint (and the subliminal message that he is a tyrant, not giving you any free air.)

20. WE ARE NEVER TOGETHER. Again, positive expressions are better than the negative. "I want to be with you more. Can you arrange it?" That will get more response from him than the exaggerated expression. Most of the time, an expression that is not really true is not well received; in this case, the word "never" takes away from the feelings he will have for your comment and ultimately it will deteriorate the relationship. Be real.

21. WE HAVE NO MONEY. This is a tough one because it happens; the month outlasts the money. If you can avoid that expression, however, it will be good for both of you. Can you say something like, "There's $25 left in the account"? If that is possible, you will find that neither of you will feel as panicked. He will reflect hope, and you will receive the benefit.

22. I NEED MORE MONEY. This sometimes is not possible; and if you ask for it when it is not available, you both hit a stressful time netting zero! If possible, lay out your needs for discussion and let him help you decide how much. When you both do it together, he has some of the "ownership" in the decisions, and you will net more for the needs you and he have agreed upon.

23. DON'T BOTHER ME TONIGHT. His reaction will be, "You mean I have been a 'bother' to you on those other nights?" Is that what I am, a bother?" If you can accommodate him, do so. If you just can't, say something like, "As much as it means to me, I am just not up to it right now. Ask again."

24. LIFE IS A DRAG. He will certainly feel you are a drag if he hears this remark from you. Also, he will feel he has not been good for you if all you can come up with is that statement. Better would be the comment,

"Thanks for being here; I need you." He then will make a valiant attempt to cheer you up and do nice things with/for you.

25. I'M BORED TO TEARS. Like the above (Number 24), this is a downer for him and you. A happy relationship downers do not make. "Stiff upper lip" is probably the order here. Appear up, make him be up, and "up" will probably happen. Boring women (or bored women) often find themselves alone.

26. DAN BOUGHT JILL FLOWERS. "What's that supposed to mean?" he'll wonder. "Did I miss something? Was I supposed to bring her flowers? Am I not sensitive." Is Dan catching her eye? At best, he is not likely to respond well even in bringing flowers to you if he thinks you had to tell him to get them. Arrange to let him see how much you love flowers by your actions when an occasion presents itself, not by words directed at him.

27. I'M HOME ALL DAY. When he is in from a hard work day, sometimes wishing he could be home, he does not really want to hear pity or a complaint or an indirect slur to get taken out. Better to say something on the order of, "Let's plan a night out later this week and have a little fun. Where do you think we could go that is

not very expensive?" That way, he has control and knows positively and above board that you are needing a night away from "the grind."

Your intent is to avoid being characterized as a "nag," and still communicate positively some of your needs and wants.

## CHAPTER THIRTY-FOUR
## SEVEN PRINCIPLES FOR MAKING LOVE

> You mustn't force sex to do the work of love or love to do the work of sex.
>
> Mary McCarthy

There is a very intimate mix of being in love and making love. Sexual intercourse within a marriage is the ideal for woman and man because all the fears and guilts, restraints and inhibitions, are removed. In marriage, the fear of STD (sexually transmitted diseases) are gone. Pregnancy is no longer a no-no. No guilt of "betraying a spouse" interferes with performance. The entire range of pleasure is not prohibited. The potential for true harmony is open to you and your man when your love has led to marriage and your intimacy is unforbidden by law, family, church, tradition, culture, or custom. You are free for the purest expressions of your love.

This chapter is to suggest several aspects of making love within the framework of love and marriage. Much of the idea of making love concerns attitude; thus, the principles associated with lovemaking as regards your mental aspect are brought into focus.

1. DO NOT BE ASHAMED. Not being ashamed is not intended to imply that you should not present yourself enticingly. It is equally acceptable (in fact, preferable) to have very low lights in the room. Modesty is still very seductive and should be practical.

The foreplay area of lovemaking will be different for virtually every couple, but being ashamed will hamper you and your man. This time will be very important and should never be rushed. Both of you should take your time; using a "slow hand," as the song says. You will adjust to each other as you get to know each other, and you will learn that the first part of making love must not be slipshod; rather, it must be new and fresh, titillating and varied, with some nice surprises by both parties.

2. DO NOT MAKE HIM FEEL ASHAMED. Your attitude toward your man's looks or words or actions are

very important in lovemaking. As in most aspects of his life, he needs acceptance, praise, and compliments. Especially are sincere comments of approval necessary in this important part of your relationship.

Any negatives during these intimate moments may, in fact, end the moment or the night! A negative word here may not just end the night; it may end a lot more. A man cannot easily forget a remark (whether serious or one made jokingly) about his looks or actions during the time he is making love or preparing to make love.

Remember, his ego is important to his performance. At these times, always be sincere, but always praise—no negative criticism—during the moments of shared love.

Never shame him or tease him; make him feel (as he really is) the man of your life!

3. LEARN WHAT HE LIKES. It is important that you learn quickly what your man likes and dislikes during your times of making love.

If you are doing something he likes, you will learn by his response. He may not tell you as he will just think you know. If he dislikes it, you can tell again by his reaction—he will pull away, avoid or resist it, although again, he may not tell you.

When you learn what he likes, make only minor variations off that positive and try to pick up on whether it is an improvement or not. If it is, be sure and repeat it, making modifications only slightly and one small step each time. You do not want to ruin a good thing.

Doing what he likes means you have to know what he likes. Patiently learn what he likes by experience and observation, realizing it may be difficult for him to say it well.

4.  LET HIM KNOW WHAT YOU LIKE. Without getting analytical and technical, let your man know what gives you pleasure during lovemaking. Again, this is best done by your response and reaction to him. Positive reinforcement will certainly encourage him to continue and repeat the acts that are good for your enjoyment.

If something is not comfortable, you must let him know. Say something like, "The (other thing) was much better for me; go back to that." That way, he is not made to feel that he goofed up. In fact, the "other thing" may give him confidence as you positively react to him again.

It's true that people vary a lot in their desire (or need) to discuss sex, but, in general, the less verbal analysis and discussion between you and yours the better. Communication during performance is the most memorable and effective.

Saying, "Yes, Yes." at the proper time is a sure way, during lovemaking, to let him know he is doing well. That way, he learns very clearly what you like.

5. OFFER YOURSELF TO HIM WHEN HE DESIRES YOU. The time may not always be to your liking; in fact, it may not be the right time, but when it is possible, you should give yourself to him.

First, this will satisfy him of his immediate need; and secondly, he will begin to adjust the timing to be appropriate for you and him. He will determine naturally when it is best for you, thus best for him.

Most men's greatest pleasure is satisfying his woman. Secondly, getting satisfaction himself follows closely. Generally, they work hand-in-hand. When he knows you are being satisfied, his satisfaction comes rather surely.

Making yourself available to him when he desires you helps him avoid frustration and disappointment and even anger.

6. LET HIM KNOW YOU EXPECT HIM TO RESPOND WHEN YOU HAVE A SEXUAL DESIRE. What is good for the gander is good for the goose. You may feel

free to expect his attentions when you have a need for sexual play or intercourse.

It is a little more difficult for him to respond sometimes than others, and certainly more difficult for him than you. Therefore, you will need to employ patience and thought to your own method of seduction. This will be a little more subtle and require more time and a proper approach.

In other words, just saying it will not do it. Coquettishness, coyness, and flirtatiousness will be the more sure course for you to take. Speaking arousal into existence most likely will not be guaranteed. A little tantalization will be more likely to lead to your "successful conquest."

7. MAINTAIN YOUR FAITHFULNESS, LOYALTY, AND FIDELITY. Generally speaking, virtue still gains its own rewards. If you are a pure woman for your husband, he is most likely to be pure for you. He surely will be more prone to feel you are his and his alone for sexual pleasure if he has trust in you.

The trust avoids jealousy and questions and accusations. As long as you maintain your purity, you will be an enticing sex partner for your man. If ever that veil of purity is torn (or doubted), the sexual act will be more difficult for him to perform with you.

When both of you are committed and dedicated to each other, the purest sex occurs and gives the ultimate pleasure.

## CHAPTER THIRTY-FIVE
## TEN QUESTIONS ABOUT FINANCES

> Ideally, couples need three lives; one for him, one for her, and one for them together.
>
> Jacqueline Bisset

One of the most important factors, if not the most important one, is finances when a permanent relationship goes on the rocks and becomes a total shipwreck. If there is enough money to cover all the needs and quite a few of the wants of a relationship, the other influences in a relationship can often be managed.

There is quite a difference in two single people making their own money and two people pooling their combined incomes and both living off it. Still there is the third possibility of one person earning all the money and both people living from it.

1. HOW IMPORTANT IS MONEY TO YOU? If you have a strong need for the things money can buy, it would not be wise for you to begin a relationship with a man who is not driven by a career that does not hold out much promise for a large amount of money. Frustration is bound to accompany a relationship where the man does not earn (in his field) the money necessary to fulfill his woman's desire and ambition.

It is a mistake by both you and the man to think either of your attitudes will change. It is not likely that any vocation will suddenly lead to a pot of gold. The percentage of people who "stumble onto" a goldmine is low and cannot be plugged into the equation.

If money and/or material things are not important to you (other than basic needs), and other things make you happy, a man who provides these essentials may offer you the life and love that lasts until "death do you part."

2. WILL YOUR MAN'S INCOME BE ENOUGH FOR YOU? You may be able to do a little study and make a few queries into the careers of people who do the work your man does and find out what their earning potential

should be.  An easy projection along with an easy-enough determination of living expenses should give you an idea of what to expect regarding income, outgo, and difference (available money for your wants).  If there is no "difference," you may want to do some more considering about love and marriage.

Not enough "difference" in the money coming in and the money going out creates stressed relationships, unhappiness, and split ups.  It is wise to be serious about finances before getting serious about marriage.  Being serious about finances only after a wedding causes serious problems in the relationship.

3. WILL YOU PLAN TO WORK FOR MORE FAMILY INCOME?  Some men still hold to the belief that they are responsible for providing the necessary income to take care of their family.  Some will not agree to a wife working, while others encourage work by their spouse.  Everything in between is acceptable by different men, who should leave it up to his woman to decide whether she works or not.

It should be discussed openly during dating days what you expect to do regarding work.  If you imply you want to provide a portion of the income and you both agree, you really impact the budget if you decide not to work.

On the other hand, you may well split your relationship apart if you do work after agreeing, before the "bond" developed, not to work. Whether you work or not must be determined before your relationship, romance, goes very far. Neither you nor your man should spring a financial surprise after you are committed to each other.

Before you go far into a relationship, discuss and agree on whether you will be working or not, and if you will, agree on the circumstances that may cause you to work—when you will start and when you will stop.

4. WHAT HAPPENS IF FINANCES RUN LOW? "For richer or poorer" is a phrase that may well be tested in a marriage relationship. One end of the wealth scale may be as disastrous to a relationship as the other. Of the two, more couples experience the "poorer" extreme.

When the money runs out before the bills are paid, it cannot just be ignored. Something happens! How do you plan to handle that? How will you view your man if he cannot pay your bills or if you two together cannot meet all financial obligations?

Will this be a time of such stress that you become at odds with each other or will you pull together to pay debts? Will you point your finger at him and his inability to provide or will you accept his accusations that you are responsible for spending too much.

Many couples work out a budget and work together to stick to it, taking out for themselves only an agreed-upon amount during a pay period.

Answer this question in advance of serious commitment.

5. WHAT IF YOUR MAN "STRIKES IT RICH" WITH EXCESS INCOME? This can be much better than the other extreme...or much worse! On the good side, if you and your man have a compatible point of view on where to spend this extra money, plan to share and enjoy.

If he comes to you and offers the opportunity to equally use the new found money, your relationship is good and you both have been doing things right. If you and he have agreed to stay together "for richer," then he is supposed to share this money with you. Either way, plan things to do with this money as you have with previous income.

Quite often, money (a lot of money) "goes to the head" of the recipient and he goes off on a "spree." If you are not included in these new ventures, look for the exit door because he is wrong and there will likely be a third party in the spree. Once that is found to be true, the game should be over. Do not stay in the game for the money; walk away with your honor and dignity fully intact.

6. WHAT IF YOU "STRIKE IT RICH" (AND HE DOES NOT)? Depending upon your previous views of finances, and assuming you had a completely agreed upon budget and program, continue as was. If you want to keep your man, discuss the extra money, get his views on how you both should view the "windfall," and proceed with a plan that suits you.

Note that this money is not his; it may be yours and his.

The man may well say that it's yours, and for you to spend it the way you choose. That's cool. Use a part of it for both of you anyway. He really will appreciate that, and the generosity will be reciprocated.

If it is up to you completely to spend it, use it well and wise. In his eyes, your stature will grow exceedingly; and his respect for you will be strengthened. That's never bad.

7. WHAT ARE THE BEST WAYS TO USE YOUR FAMILY INCOME? Always, planning is better than not planning. There are men who like to detail their plans, others who like "broad-brush," general directions and budgets, and others who never think about budgeting programs and just blow and go spending daily and loosely.

You will fit into the plan somewhere (near the middle is what your author would select). If you are a better budgeter and treasurer than he is, and he is content to have you do the planning, paying, and spending, you may feel obliged to do so. The better you handle the money, the more content he will be with your management. You then determine how the family income is used.

The budget should generally fall into something like the following:

    Constants that must be paid.
    Unconstants that must be paid.
    Savings (short term)
    Savings (long term for emergencies)
    Wants high priority
    Wants (if anything is left over)

With this budget plan, you make car, house, and utility payments under "constants." Credit cards are paid under "unconstants." You buy things for house, home, and family under "high priority wants." Personal miscellaneous (for you and your man) fall under "leftover wants." You save for emergencies, or something like a vacation or a new car under "short term savings." And, you save for retirement, college for kids, new home, or business under "long term savings."

If you can lay all these things out together, control the "wants," you will have a very secure and comfortable man.

8. WHO IS RESPONSIBLE FOR FAMILY EXPENDITURES? It is wise for you and your man to have agreement on all expenditures in the general budget and up to a limited amount per designated period. For example, without his okay, you spend X number of dollars during Y number of days (or weeks or per month); and so does he. Above the designated amount or in less than the specified number of days, you again agree on the expense in question before you or he spends the money.

It is a terrific idea to have three areas of responsibility—yours, his, and both. From "both" comes the "must be paids"; while from the "wants" (if anything is left over) comes "your allowance" and "his allowance" to be spent by each other with no obligation to tell the other where it went. Here is another good opportunity for both of you to buy something for the other.

9. HOW CAN YOU EQUITABLY DIVIDE THE FAMILY INCOME? If it is agreed that all the income goes into one common account to be used from by both of you, the money can be managed well. In order to divide the money to both your satisfaction, the division must come from the "wants" portion.

With that established, you both should want to discuss your respective uses of the money, which may be gifts, coffee money, lunch money, golfing money, bowling money, art class, etc., et al. After you both discuss all contingencies that can come up under your "allowances," get sincere agreement that you will take and use that amount only, every period.

Stick with it. If you run out of money before the time period is up, just wait for the next period. One word for the wise—do not borrow against the future allowance. That will cause trouble.

10. **WHEN ONE OF YOU OVEREXTENDS EXPENSES, HOW IS IT TO BE RESOLVED?** If you can imagine situations that may arise where you might spend more than you have (or at least have more bills than you have salary), talk about ways to resolve the problem. Get each other's views on borrowing from lending institutions, running up the credit cards, withdrawing from savings, borrowing from family or friends, working overtime, working part time, taking on "several" jobs, any other activity affecting money (even gambling, investing lottery), and finally, bankruptcy.

It is important that you know his views in advance about all these matters. Just as wisely, you should let him know your ideas.

Once you are "over budget," work together to "dig out." Again, finger-pointing will clear no bills. Use the occasion to learn and plan how not to let it happen again. Without criticism or accusations, work out the problem together. The questions are, "How did we let this happen? How can we prevent it from happening again?"

Finances split more homes, marriages, and relationships than problems of sex, infidelity, or incompatibility; although Groucho Marx used to say, "His income was not enough, and her compatibility was not enough." Whenever matters of finance arise, they must be worked out together. Neither side should take all the blame nor place all blame on the other. Rework something to get back to a comfortable zone.

## CHAPTER THIRTY-SIX
## FOUR VIEWS ON LOVE HELD BY MOST MEN

...Love from one being to another can only be that two solitudes come nearer, recognize and protect and comfort each other.

Han Suyin (Mrs. Elizabeth Comber)

A man is an extremely complicated creature. Although women have always been thought of as emotionally complex and men as shallow, plain, and easy-to-see-through, it is this author's conclusion that both sexes are not simple, not totally definable nor knowable.

These few lines are intended to give a man's view of love, his approach to love, his view of sex appeal, and his approach to sex. These are all basic and exceptions will exist, but they are not the stereotypical male with his "brains between his legs."

Certainly, the man is made mentally to "see" women. It is surely true that he can have base thoughts about a woman and a "relationship" with her, but he does hold a view of love that is as deep and sensitive as that of a woman. It may be, probably is, different than the view of a woman, but it can (usually does) drive him to be better.

One seminar leader of Male-Female Relationships described men as like lights, on and off with the flip of a switch. Women, he said, were like irons, slow to warm up, and slow to cool down. No one would deny the truth of these comparisons, but one could say that both sexes can learn and understand these facts. Once understood, the knowledge can help relationships be strong and lasting.

The point is then that any man can live and behave and talk and think in such a way as to be well worthy of a woman's love. The following paragraphs are the words of a man.

1. A MAN'S VIEW OF LOVE. Love is when one heart embraces another. When one person shares

everything—sorrow and joy—with another. When talk is open and free, and no subject is "off limit."

When one would literally die for another. When one puts another before one's own feelings, health, comfort, thirst, hunger, breath of life. When one will do all to care for and help another.

When emptiness of absence and separation hurts so bad, one will do anything to be with another. When no score is kept of the good things one does for the other or the bad things one does to the other.

Love is when sex is not a goal of conquest, but becomes a mutual act of pleasure and excitement and satisfaction. When one attempts to meet and satisfy the need of the other.

Love offers the freedom of each one to be oneself truly and wholly in the presence of the other.

2. A MAN'S APPROACH TO LOVE. A man feels! He has feelings and emotion! He can be touched and moved and made to hurt and cry. He feels with his heart and with his mind and with his soul.

When he does something wrong or hurtful or sinful, he can be penitent, and he can apologize and say he is sorry—and feel it and mean it. He does not necessarily think it is "unmanly" to be apologetic.

## Donald Petty

He can be brought to his knees by an act of heroism or patriotism or kindness. He can become emotional inside and outside by thoughts of kindnesses and favors and acts of genuine love and caring.

A thought occurred to one long-married man summed up in one number—"14,965." The number has great significance in the life of the man for it is the number of pairs of socks that his wife had folded for him in forty-one years of marriage—one pair per day!

His thoughts were of socks, but he knew it meant countless other acts of love given freely and forgotten, not counted, not put on permanent records, not considered as a score or debt or obligation. Just given of a free will, loving heart, and generous spirit.

How then could that man approach love in an abusive or selfish way? He did work hard to provide the warmth and shelter, encouragement and honor, respect and praise, love and sexual satisfaction for his wife of all those years.

The approach of the man matched that of the woman, substance not image or words. He tried to use the right approach of love and trust and sharing and giving to reciprocate her devotion, loyalty, and understanding given so liberally over all those years.

As selfish and egotistical as a man might be, when a virtuous, patient, long-suffering woman gives cheerfully of herself, he is capable of as much love and tenderness as she. He will come through in time, for a woman who is wise enough to give and hold on.

3. A MAN'S VIEW OF SEX APPEAL. That rare quality when a properly developed body combines with the appropriate beauty in the eyes, mouth, hair, and entire face and correct personality that communicates interest in another without actually speaking.

When one with true sex appeal does speak, the voice is pleasant and not clamorous. The words are not silly and not pretentious; rather, they are genuine, sincere, and meaningful.

The look, action, speech, and appearance when sitting, standing lying, or walking are elegant and sophisticated. An entrance of one with true sex appeal "lights up a room," turns heads, and raises the level of interest in everyone.

The one with true sex appeal is not cheap, does not convey raucousness or bawdiness, does not intentionally or consciously cause lust of only a sexual nature.

Purity and innocence accompany real sex appeal.

Donald Petty

4. A MAN'S APPROACH TO SEX. Not all men are selfish lovers when it comes to sex. When sex is a wholesome approach, the man knows that a woman prefers the pure sexual intercourse of a husband.

There are exceptions to this "ideal" by man and woman. It is recognized that some may not consider sex outside the marriage bonds to be wrong or harmful. Your author considers it a violation of marriage vows or a breaking of biblical standards for a single person. Whoever does commit, then, illicit sex has broken a law of one kind or another.

Given the above, a man's approach to sex is an enjoyable act to him with the objective of making it an enjoyable act for the woman. An idea period of lovemaking is the time for a man and woman to fully enjoy foreplay leading to a completely fulfilling act, and finishing with a satisfying time of caressing and intimate togetherness long after the act.

It is not a simple physical act, but a mutual time of expressing love mentally, verbally, physically, unselfishly, and satisfactorily for both. The totality of the act requires the concentration of the man dedicated to raising every fiber of the woman's makeup to a high pitch of excitement and a satisfying attention to every emotion she feels.

The man's approach to sex is to answer every sexual need of the woman. To this he will be dedicated when the love is there and true.

It is felt that women must initiate the dialogue with regard to a man's interests before the man learns how to return that care and attention. In the long run, however, with the ground work done and the foundation laid correctly by the woman, the man will complete the structure of a strong, durable, lifelong relationship.

*Donald Petty*

For the quotes at the chapter beginnings, the author thanks THE QUOTABLE WOMAN. Philadelphia, PA: Running Press, 1991.

## ABOUT THE AUTHOR

Don Petty is an internationally-know speaker, having given over 50 speeches or lectures during the period 2001-2003, while additionally working full time as chief consultant and president of the company he founded in 1991, LINE OF SNACKS Consultants International.

Before the fall of the Shah of Iran in 1979. Mr. Petty worked as a mathematics teacher in Teheran, Iran, and was there the day the Shah Reza Pahlavi left Iran for the last time. Two days after the Ayatolloah Khomeini returned to Iran in February 1979, from his exile in France. Mr. Petty hastily departed the country.

His 1956 marriage to Sylvia Flippin, who was the daughter of a late East Texas cattleman, gave them a son and three daughters and ten grandchildren. The Pettys reside in Dallas, Texas.